Natalie King, Sam Holyman and Claire

ESSENTIALS

OCR Gateway
GCSE Science B
Revision Guide

Contents

Contents

Physics

Fundamental Scientific Processes

Scientists carry out **experiments** and collect **evidence** in order to explain how and why things happen. Scientific knowledge and understanding can lead to the **development of new technologies** which have a huge impact on **society** and the **environment**.

Scientific evidence is often based on data that has been collected through **observations** and **measurements**. To allow scientists to reach conclusions, evidence must be **repeatable**, **reproducible** and **valid**.

Models

Models are used to explain scientific ideas and the universe around us. Models can be used to describe:
- a complex idea like how heat moves through a metal
- a system like the Earth's structure.

Models make a system or idea easier to understand by only including the most important parts. They can be used to explain real world observations or to make predictions. But, because models don't contain all the **variables**, they do sometimes make incorrect predictions.

Models and scientific ideas may change as new observations are made and new **data** are collected. Data and observations may be collected from a series of experiments. For example, the accepted model of the structure of the atom has been modified as new technology and further experiments have produced new evidence.

Hypotheses

Scientific explanations are called **hypotheses**. Hypotheses are used to explain observations. A hypothesis can be tested by planning experiments and collecting data and evidence. For example, if you pull a metal wire you may observe that it stretches. This can be explained by the scientific idea that the atoms in the metal are in layers and can slide over each other. A hypothesis can be modified as new data is collected, and may even be disproved.

Data

Data can be displayed in **tables**, **pie charts** or **line graphs**. In your exam you may be asked to:
- choose the most appropriate method for displaying data
- identify trends
- use the data mathematically, including using statistical methods, calculating the **mean** and calculating gradients on graphs.

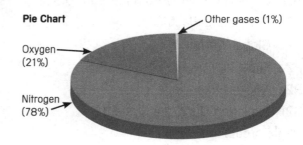

Pie Chart

Other gases (1%)
Oxygen (21%)
Nitrogen (78%)

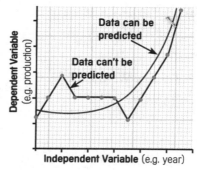

Line Graph

Data can be predicted
Data can't be predicted

Dependent Variable (e.g. production)

Independent Variable (e.g. year)

Table

Pressure (Atmospheres)	Yield (%) Temperature (°C)			
	250	350	450	550
200	73	50	28	13
400	77	65	45	26

Data (Cont.)

Sometimes the same data can lead to different conclusions. For example, data shows that the world's average temperatures have been rising significantly over the last 200 years. Some scientists think this is due to increased combustion of fossil fuels, whilst other scientists think it's a natural change seen before in Earth's history.

Scientific and Technological Development

Every scientific or technological development could have effects that we do not know about. This can give rise to **issues**. An issue is an important question that is in dispute and needs to be settled. Issues could be:

- **Social** – they impact on the human population of a community, city, country, or the world.
- **Environmental** – they impact on the planet, its natural ecosystems and resources.
- **Economic** – money and related factors like employment and the distribution of resources.
- **Cultural** – what is morally right and wrong; a value judgement must be made.

Peer review is a process of self-regulation involving experts in a particular field who **critically examine** the work undertaken. Peer review methods are designed to maintain standards and provide **credibility** for the work that has been carried out. The methods used vary depending on the type of work and also on the overall purpose behind the review process.

Evaluating Information

Conclusions can then be made based on the scientific evidence that has been collected and should try to explain the results and observations.

Evaluations look at the whole investigation. It is important to be able to evaluate information relating to social-scientific issues. When evaluating information:

- make a list of **pluses** (pros)
- make a list of **minuses** (cons)
- consider how each point might **impact on society**.

You also need to consider whether the source of information is reliable and credible and consider opinions, bias and weight of evidence.

Opinions are personal viewpoints. Opinions backed up by valid and reliable evidence carry far more weight than those based on non-scientific ideas. Opinions of experts can also carry more weight than opinions of non-experts. Information is **biased** if it favours one particular viewpoint without providing a balanced account. Biased information might include incomplete evidence or try to influence how you interpret the evidence.

B1 Fitness and Health

The Circulatory System

Your **circulatory system** carries oxygen and glucose in your blood to all your body's cells so that energy can be released through **aerobic respiration**.

Your **heart** pumps blood around your body:
- Your heart **relaxes** to fill with blood.
- Your heart **contracts** to squeeze the blood out into the **arteries**.

When the heart contracts, the blood is put under pressure and is sent into the arteries. This ensures that the blood reaches all parts of the body supplying cells with glucose and oxygen for respiration. This surge of blood is the **heart beat** or **pulse**. Blood in the arteries is always under pressure.

Heart

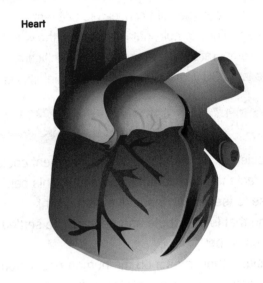

Blood Pressure

Blood pressure is a measure of the force of blood per unit area as it flows through the arteries. It's measured in **mm Hg (millimetres of mercury)**.

Blood pressure is represented by two measurements, e.g. 120/80 mm Hg:
- **Systolic** blood pressure (the first number) is the pressure in your arteries when your heart contracts, i.e. when blood pressure is at its highest.
- **Diastolic** blood pressure (the second number) is the pressure in your arteries when your heart relaxes.

Normal blood pressure is about 120/80 mm Hg. But, it can be affected by age and lifestyle.

You can reduce high blood pressure and maintain normal blood pressure by doing regular aerobic exercise to strengthen your heart. A healthy diet can also help by keeping weight steady.

Factors that can lead to high blood pressure include:
- Excess weight – the circulatory system has to work harder to pump blood around the body of a person who is overweight.
- High stress levels.
- Excess alcohol.

- A diet which is high in saturated fat, sugar and / or salt. Too much salt can raise blood pressure, whilst too much **saturated fat** can lead to a build-up of **cholesterol** in the arteries forming plaques. The amount of cholesterol in arteries can be linked to the amount of saturated fat eaten. This plaque bulges into the lumen, restricting or blocking blood flow through the arteries, increasing the risk of heart attack.
- Smoking – the carbon monoxide produced reduces the oxygen-carrying capacity of the blood so the heart rate and pressure increases in order to compensate. Plus, nicotine increases the heart rate.

(HT) Carbon monoxide takes the place of oxygen in the haemoglobin so the oxygen-carrying capacity of the blood is greatly reduced.

Blood Pressure (Cont.)

In the long-term, **high blood pressure** is dangerous because the blood vessels can weaken and eventually burst. If a blood vessel bursts in the brain it may lead to brain damage or a stroke. In the kidneys it may lead to kidney damage.

Low blood pressure means the blood doesn't circulate efficiently, so some parts of the body are deprived of **glucose** and oxygen. This can lead to dizziness, fainting, and cold hands and feet. Pressure may drop in the kidneys, leading to kidney failure.

Causes of Heart Disease

Many factors increase the risk of **heart disease**:

- High blood pressure.
- Smoking – carbon monoxide combines with red blood cells, preventing them from carrying as much oxygen.
- Too much salt.
- High-fat diets.

High-fat diets and high cholesterol can block arteries and cause heart attacks. Heart attacks are more likely with narrowed coronary arteries and thrombosis.

Health and Fitness

Being **healthy** means being free from infection (i.e. no coughs, colds or diseases).

Being **fit** relates to how much physical activity you're capable of doing and how quickly your body recovers afterwards.

Different types of exercise develop different aspects of fitness, all of which are measurable. For example, strength, stamina, flexibility, agility and speed can all be measured.

Cardiovascular efficiency – how well your heart copes with aerobic exercise and how quickly it recovers afterwards – is often used as a measure of general fitness.

A fit person's heart will return to its normal resting rate much quicker than a less fit person's heart. During exercise, a fitter person will have a lower heart rate than a less fit person.

There are many ways to measure fitness. It is best to use a combination of tests, rather than just one, when making decisions on how fit someone is.

B1 Human Health and Diet

A Balanced Diet

Food supplies living organisms with **energy** and **nutrients**. A balanced diet must contain:

- **carbohydrates** and **fats** to provide energy
- **protein** for growth and repair of tissues (and energy, if carbohydrates are in short supply).

Carbohydrates are made of simple sugars such as glucose. **Fats** are made up of fatty acids and glycerol. **Proteins** are made up of **amino acids**.

(HT) Carbohydrates are stored in the liver as glycogen or can be converted to fats. Fats are stored under the skin and around organs as adipose tissue. Proteins are not stored.

Although they don't provide energy, you also need other substances in your diet to keep your body **healthy**, including:

- **minerals**, e.g. iron to make haemoglobin in red blood cells
- **vitamins**, e.g. vitamin C to prevent scurvy

- **fibre** to prevent constipation and to maintain healthy bowels.
- **water** to prevent dehydration, and to help remove waste.

You might alter your diet as a result of:

- **beliefs** about animal welfare, e.g. vegetarians, vegans
- **religious beliefs**, e.g. the Muslim and Jewish faiths prohibit the eating of pig meat
- **medical issues**, and food allergies, e.g. some people are allergic to peanuts
- **age** – older people need less food (fewer calories); younger people need more calories (as they are more active) and more protein
- **sex** – males need more calories due to being larger and having more muscle
- **activity** – someone with a physical job, e.g. a builder, will need more calories than an office worker
- **personal choice**.

How Much Energy is Needed?

The amount of **energy** you need depends on your age, sex and activity levels.

To maintain a healthy **body mass**, you must **balance** the amount of energy you consume with the amount of energy you use up through daily activity.

You can calculate your **Body Mass Index (BMI)** using this formula:

$$BMI = \frac{Mass\ (kg)}{Height\ (m)^2}$$

Then you can find your BMI in the chart to see what it means.

BMI	What it Means
<18.5	Underweight (too light for your height)
18.5–24.9	Ideal weight (correct weight for your height)
25-29.9	Overweight (too heavy for your height)
>30	Obese (much too heavy; health risks)

If you consume more food than you need, you will become very overweight or obese.

Obesity is a major health problem in the developed world. It can lead to arthritis (swollen and painful joints), heart disease, type II **diabetes** and breast cancer.

Nutrients • Carbohydrate • Fats • Protein

Protein

Protein molecules are long chains of **amino acids**.

(HT) • **Essential** amino acids must be taken in by eating food (your body can't make them).
• **Non-essential** amino acids can be made in your body.

Protein supplies the nutrients that enable you to grow. This is why it's important for teenagers to have a high-protein diet.

(HT) Proteins from animal origin are called **first class proteins**. Meat and fish are first class proteins because they contain all the essential amino acids (which cannot be made by the body). Plant proteins are called second class proteins.

In some parts of the world (i.e. developing countries), food is in very short supply, so people don't get enough protein in their diet.

In children, protein **deficiency** results in a disease called **kwashiorkor**. This disease is common in developing countries due to overpopulation and limited investment in agriculture.

You can calculate your **estimated average daily requirement** for protein (**EAR**) using this formula:

$$EAR = 0.6 \times Body\ mass\ (kg)$$

Protein is only used as an energy source when carbohydrates or fats are not available.

(HT) EAR is an estimated daily figure for an average person of a certain body mass. It can vary depending on age, pregnancy and lactation (i.e. whether a woman is producing milk).

Poor Diets and Eating Disorders

Low self-esteem, poor self-image and a desire for perfection can all lead to a poor diet.

Poor diets can be very damaging to the body. The body doesn't get the balance of energy and nutrients needed to function correctly. The reproduction system may be affected as well as damage to the bones.

Eating disorders such as anorexia nervosa or bulimia nervosa may result.

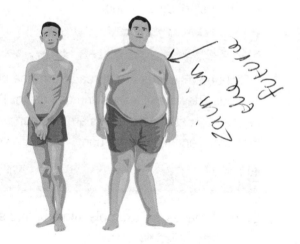

Quick Test

1. What factors affect blood pressure?
2. How can you calculate your BMI?
3. What diseases are linked to obesity?
4. Why is kwashiorkor mainly found in developing countries?

Key Words   Amino acids • Deficiency • Kwashiorkor

Non-Infectious Diseases

Non-infectious diseases can't be caught from another person. There are many causes:

- **Poor diet**, e.g. a lack of vitamin C causes scurvy, and a lack of iron causes anaemia.
- **Organ malfunction**, e.g. the pancreas stops producing insulin (which causes diabetes).

- **Genetic inheritance**, e.g. people inherit the genes for a particular disease from their parent, e.g. red–green colour blindness.
- **Cells mutate** and become **cancerous**.

These diseases are different to infectious diseases in that they can't be 'caught' or passed on. No **pathogens** are involved.

Cancer

Cancer is a **non-infectious** disease where cells grow out of control and form tumours.

Making healthy lifestyle choices is one way to reduce the likelihood of getting cancer, for example:

- Don't smoke – chemicals in cigarettes cause lung cancer and other cancers like throat cancer.
- Don't drink excess alcohol – alcohol is linked to cancer of the liver, gut and mouth.
- Avoid getting sunburn – skin cells damaged by the sun can become cancerous.
- Eat a healthy diet – a high-fibre diet can reduce the risk of bowel cancer.

HT Cancerous cells divide in an abnormal and uncontrolled way, forming lumps of cells called **tumours**.

A tumour that grows in one place is described as benign. But, if cells break off and secondary tumours start to grow in other parts of the body, the tumour is described as malignant.

A person's chance of **survival** depends on the type of cancer they have. The chance of survival is greater if the cancer is diagnosed early, the patient is young and the tumour is benign.

Infectious Diseases

Infectious diseases are spread from one person to another. They are diseases you can catch. They are caused by **pathogens**, which are **microorganisms** that attack and invade the body.

Examples include fungi, viruses, bacteria and protozoa. For example, athlete's foot is caused by a fungus, flu is caused by a virus, cholera is caused by a bacterium and malaria is caused by a protozoan.

Malaria

Some diseases, for example, **malaria**, are spread by organisms called **vectors**:

1. A mosquito (the **vector**) sucks blood from a human (the **host** where the vectors live).
2. If there are malaria **parasites** (organisms that live off other organisms) in the blood, they mate and move from the mosquito's gut to its salivary glands.
3. The mosquito bites another person and passes the malaria parasites into their bloodstream.

4. The malaria parasites move to the liver, where they mature and reproduce.
5. The new generation of malaria parasites migrates to the blood and replicates in red blood cells, bursting them open. This damage leads to characteristic malaria fever and can sometimes result in death.

HT Malaria (Cont.)

Knowledge of the life cycle of a disease and the way in which vectors spread the disease can help in controlling it. For example, malaria can be prevented by controlling the vector (the mosquito) by:

- sleeping under mosquito nets
- using insect repellents
- killing mosquitoes with insecticide.

By taking these precautions, the spread of the disease is greatly reduced.

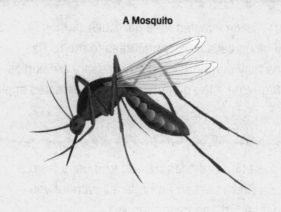

A Mosquito

Defences Against Pathogens

The body has a number of **defences** to stop pathogens getting in:

- The **skin** acts as a barrier against microorganisms.
- The **blood clots** in wounds to prevent microorganisms from entering the bloodstream.

- The **respiratory system** is lined with cells that produce a sticky, liquid mucus that forms a mucus membrane to trap microorganisms.
- The **stomach** produces **hydrochloric acid** which kills microorganisms in the food we eat.

Dealing with Pathogens Inside the Body

If **pathogens** enter the body, **white blood cells** start fighting the invasion. The symptoms of a disease are caused by **pathogens** damaging cells and **producing** toxins (poisons) before the white blood cells can destroy them.

There are two types of white blood cell, which deal with pathogens in two ways:

- By engulfing and digesting pathogens they find in the bloodstream.
- By making **antibodies** to attack pathogens. They recognise markers (**antigens**) on the surface of the pathogen and produce antibodies which lock onto the markers (antigens), killing the pathogens.

HT Every pathogen has **unique antigens** (markers). White blood cells make **antibodies** specifically for a particular antigen, e.g. antibodies made to fight tetanus have no effect on whooping cough or cholera.

A White Blood Cell Making Antibodies

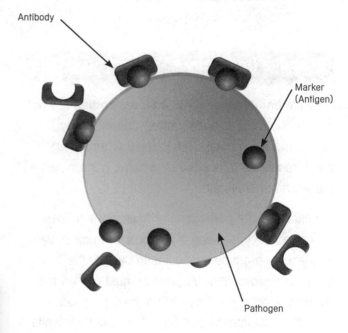

Antibody

Marker (Antigen)

Pathogen

Natural (Active) Immunity

If you've been infected by a particular **pathogen**, your white blood cells make **antibodies** to them. This means they can produce the necessary antibodies much quicker if the same pathogen is detected again.

This provides future **protection** against the disease and is called **natural** or **active immunity**.

The antibodies stay in the blood for years to fight future infections.

Immunisation/Vaccination

Immunisation provides natural immunity from a disease (from certain pathogens), without you being infected and becoming ill.

(HT) Immunisation (vaccination) works as follows:

1. A person is **injected** with a weakened or dead strain of the pathogen, which is incapable of multiplying. It's harmless.
2. Even though the pathogens are harmless, the antigens (markers) **trigger** the production of specific **antibodies** by the white blood cells.
3. Long after the pathogen has been dealt with, the white blood cells remain **in the blood** (memory cells are produced). This means more antibodies can be produced very quickly if the same pathogen is detected again.

Benefits of immunisation:

- It **protects** against diseases which could kill or cause disability, e.g. polio, measles.
- If everybody is vaccinated, the disease can't spread and eventually **dies out**. (This is what happened to smallpox.)

Risks of immunisation:

- An individual could have a **bad reaction** to the vaccine.
- No vaccination is 100% safe, but the benefits outweigh the risks.

Passive Immunity

Passive immunity occurs when **antibodies** are put into an individual's body, rather than the body producing them itself. This is used when a very quick response is needed or when a person has a weak immune system.

For example, the **pathogens** or **toxins** in a snake's venom act very fast, and a person's immune system is unable to produce antibodies to destroy the pathogen quickly enough, so they must be injected with antibodies. But, they will not have long-term protection against the pathogen because their white blood cells didn't produce the antibodies themselves. After a while, they will have no antibodies for that antigen left in their blood.

Treating Diseases with Drugs

Diseases caused by bacteria or fungi (not viruses) can be treated using **antibiotics**. These chemicals kill bacteria and fungi.

Antiviral drugs are used to treat diseases caused by viruses only.

(HT) Antibiotics are very effective at killing bacteria. But, if doctors over-prescribe antibiotics, all the bacteria in a population are killed off except the **resistant** ones, which then spread. So, the antibiotic then becomes useless.

MRSA is a bacteria which has become resistant to most antibiotics, making it a dangerous microorganism that the media has dubbed a '**superbug**'.

Careful use of antibiotics is needed to prevent more resistant bacterial infections occurring.

Testing New Drugs

New drugs have to be tested to make sure that they are effective and safe before they can be made available to the public.

A drug can be tested using:

- **computer models** to predict how it will affect cells, based on known information about how the body works and the effects of similar drugs
- **animals** to see how it affects living organisms (many people object on the grounds of animal cruelty)
- **human tissue** (grown in a laboratory) to see how it affects human cells. (Some people object to human tissue being grown in this way because they believe it's unnatural and wrong.)

Finally, the drug must be tested on **healthy volunteers**, and on **volunteers** who have the **disease**. Some are given the new drug and some are given a **placebo** (an inactive pill). The effects of the drug can then be compared to the effects of taking the placebo.

Although scientists conduct lots of tests beforehand to determine how the drugs will affect humans, drug trials like these can never be completely safe.

(HT) In a **blind trial**, the volunteers don't know whether they have been given the new drug or the placebo. This eliminates any psychological factors and helps to provide a fair comparison.

In a **double blind trial**, neither the volunteers nor the doctors know which pill has been given. This eliminates all bias from the test, because the doctors can't influence the volunteers' responses in any way.

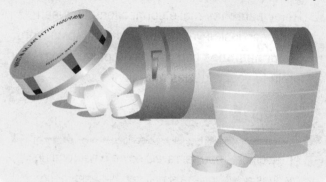

Quick Test

1. Give three examples of pathogens.
2. (HT) Briefly describe immunisation (vaccination).
3. (HT) How can you prevent the spread of malaria?

B1 The Nervous System

The Nervous System

Your **nervous system** allows you to **react** to your surroundings and **coordinate** your behaviour. It comprises the **central nervous system** (CNS) and the **peripheral nervous system** (PNS), which includes receptors and neurones.

Animals detect changes in their environment (**stimuli**) using **receptors**, specialised nerve endings that generate nerve impulses. You have:

- light receptors in your eyes
- sound receptors and balance receptors in your ears
- taste receptors on your tongue
- smell receptors in your nose
- touch, pressure, pain and temperature receptors in your skin.

The Main Components of the Nervous System

Brain

Spinal cord

The neurones that make up the peripheral nervous system

CNS (brain and spinal cord)

Neurones

Neurones (nerve cells) are specially adapted cells that can carry a **nerve impulse**. Nerve impulses are electrical messages/signals and are carried along the **axon** (the long, thin part of the cell).

There are three types of neurone:

- **Sensory neurones** carry nerve impulses from the receptors to your brain.
- **Relay neurones** make connections between neurones inside your brain and your spinal cord.
- **Motor neurones** carry nerve impulses from your brain to your muscles and glands.

A Motor Neurone

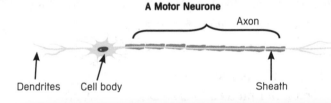

Axon

Dendrites   Cell body   Sheath

(HT) Neurones are adapted to their job. They have:

- an **elongated** (long) **shape** (axon) to make connections from one part of the body to another
- an **insulating sheath** to speed up the nerve impulse
- **dendrites** (branched endings) to allow a single neurone to act on many muscle fibres.

(HT) Synapses

1. An electrical impulse travels down a neurone until it reaches a synapse (a small gap between neurones).
2. A transmitter substance diffuses across the synapse (gap).
3. The transmitter binds with receptor molecules on the next neurone, causing an electrical impulse to be initiated in that neurone. The message goes:

Neurone A → **Synapse** → **Neurone B**
(Electrical message)   (Chemical message)   (Electrical message)

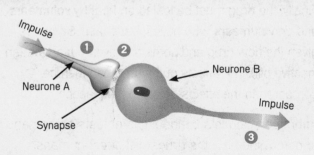

Impulse

Neurone A

Neurone B

Synapse

Impulse

Receptor • Neurone • Synapse

Voluntary Actions and Reflex Actions

Voluntary actions are under the **conscious** control of your brain, i.e. **you decide** how to react to a stimulus. For example, tasting something bitter (stimulus) and spitting it out (response).

Reflex actions (or involuntary responses) **bypass** your brain to give fast, **automatic** responses to a stimulus, to help protect your body from harm, e.g:

- pupil reflex automatically controls light entering your eye (to prevent damage to your retina)
- knee jerk reaction
- automatically withdrawing your hand from a hot plate to prevent you from getting burned.

The pathway that the message takes is called the **reflex arc**.

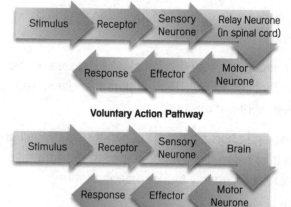

Reflex Action Pathway (Reflex Arc)

Stimulus → Receptor → Sensory Neurone → Relay Neurone (in spinal cord)

Response ← Effector ← Motor Neurone

Voluntary Action Pathway

Stimulus → Receptor → Sensory Neurone → Brain

Response ← Effector ← Motor Neurone

The Eye

Your **iris** (the coloured part of the eye) controls the amount of light that enters your eye. The rays of **light** are **refracted** by your **cornea**, and the **lens** focuses light onto the **retina** so the rays **converge** (come together) at a single point and produce a clear **image** on your retina. The light-sensitive receptor cells on your retina then cause nerve impulses to pass along sensory neurones in the **optic nerve** to your brain. The retina contains the light-sensitive receptors. Some are sensitive to colour.

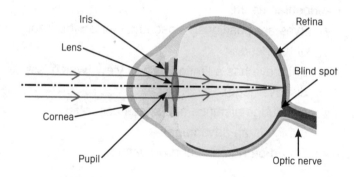

Labels: Iris, Lens, Cornea, Pupil, Retina, Blind spot, Optic nerve

(HT) The **lens** is a clear, flexible bag of fluid surrounded by circular **ciliary** muscles that change the shape of the lens (accommodation). **Suspensory** ligaments attach the lens to the ciliary muscles.

When receiving light rays from a near object:
- the ciliary muscles contract
- the suspensory ligaments relax
- the lens is short and fat to refract light a lot.

When receiving light rays from a distant object:
- the ciliary muscles relax
- the suspensory ligaments contract
- the lens is long and thin because the light only needs to be refracted a little.

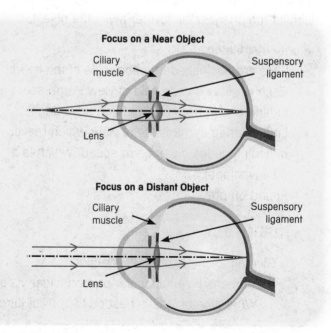

Focus on a Near Object

Labels: Ciliary muscle, Lens, Suspensory ligament

Focus on a Distant Object

Labels: Ciliary muscle, Lens, Suspensory ligament

B1 The Nervous System

Eye Defects

Common eye defects are:

- long sight
- short sight
- red–green colour blindness (an inherited condition).

In people with red–green colour blindness, some of the specialised cells in the retina that detect red and green light are missing.

Long and short sight are caused by the eyeball or the lens being the wrong **shape**, so the light rays can't be accurately **focused** on the retina.

(HT) Long and short sight can be corrected by contact lenses, glasses, or laser surgery. Long sight can be corrected by wearing a convex lens and short sight can be corrected by wearing a concave lens.

Corrective laser eye surgery works by cutting a flap in the cornea, folding it back and using a laser to reshape the cornea. With the shape of the cornea corrected, clear vision is returned and the light rays are now accurately focused on the retina.

Types of Vision

Binocular vision:

- Eyes are positioned close together on the front of the head.
- Each eye has a limited field of view (which is a disadvantage).
- Can judge distance and speed accurately (which is an advantage).
- Found on humans and predators.

The brain uses binocular vision to judge distances by comparing the images from each eye. The more similar the images, the further away the object.

Monocular vision:

- Eyes are positioned on either side of the head.
- Each eye has a wide field of view – can see behind and in front (which is an advantage).
- Little overlap in the fields of view which makes it difficult to judge distance or speed (which is a disadvantage).
- Found on prey.

Binocular Vision

Monocular Vision

Quick Test

1. Give an example of a reflex action.
2. Do humans have binocular or monocular vision?
3. (HT) What type of lens is needed to correct long sight?

Key Words   **Binocular • Monocular**

Drugs

Drugs are **chemicals** that affect your mind or body. All **beneficial** drugs, i.e. medicines, are **legal**. But some medicines can have bad side effects if not used correctly, which is why they're only available on prescription. Most **harmful** drugs are **illegal**.

Drugs are **categorised** according to the effects they produce when taken:

- **Stimulants** (e.g. caffeine, nicotine, ecstasy) increase brain activity which leads to a feeling of alertness and heightened perception.
- **Depressants** (e.g. alcohol, solvents, tranquillisers like temazepam) decrease brain activity which makes you feel tired, and slows down your reactions. It can lead to a feeling of lethargy and forgetfulness.
- **Painkillers** or anaesthetics (e.g. aspirin, Paracetamol, heroin) reduce pain by blocking nerve impulses.
- **Performance-enhancing drugs** (e.g. anabolic steroids) increase muscle development, which is why they're sometimes abused by sports people.
- **Hallucinogens** (e.g. LSD) distort what is seen and heard.

(HT) Stimulants and depressants act on the synapses of the nervous system. Stimulants cause more neuro-transmitters to cross the synapse. This speeds up the nervous impulses.

Depressants bind with receptor molecules in the membrane of the next neurone, blocking the transmission of the impulse. This slows everything down.

In the UK, illegal drugs are classified into three main categories under the Misuse of Drugs Act:

- **Class A** drugs (e.g. heroin, cocaine) are the most dangerous and carry heavy prison sentences and fines for possession.
- **Class B** drugs (including amphetamines, e.g. speed and barbiturates) have lower penalties.
- **Class C** drugs (e.g. tranquilisers and anabolic steroids) are less dangerous and have the lowest penalties.

Addiction and Rehabilitation

Drug **addiction** is a state of psychological or physical need for a drug. As an addict's body becomes more used to the drug, it develops a **tolerance** to it, i.e. the addict needs higher doses of the drug to get the same effects.

When a drug addict stops taking a drug they can suffer from **withdrawal** symptoms, including:

- **psychological** problems, e.g. cravings
- **physical** problems, e.g. sweating, shaking, nausea.

Rehabilitation is the process by which an addict learns to live without the drug. This takes a long time because their body and mind both have to adapt.

Alcohol

Drinking **excess** **alcohol** can lead to unconsciousness and even coma or death.

Short-term effects of drinking alcohol include:
- lack of balance and muscle control
- blurred vision and slurred speech
- poor judgement and drowsiness
- vasodilation – the blood vessels widen, increasing blood flow to skin and heat loss.

Long-term effects of drinking alcohol include:
- liver damage, due to the liver working very hard to remove the **toxic** alcohol from the body
- brain damage due to dehydration.

(HT) The liver contains enzymes which break down alcohol. But, the products of breakdown are toxic and cause liver damage.

Cirrhosis of the liver (i.e. damage to the liver as a result of liver disease) is a common disease amongst heavy drinkers.

The legal blood alcohol content limit for driving is 80 milligrams of alcohol per 100 millilitres of blood. This limit has been set because alcohol slows reaction times, increasing the chance of accidents. The limit is even less for aeroplane pilots.

Tobacco

Smoking can lead to several diseases, including **cancer** of the mouth, throat, oesophagus and lungs, heart disease, **emphysema** and bronchitis. Smoking damages the **cilia** (ciliated epithelial cells), which line the airways (**trachea**, **bronchi** and **bronchioles**). This prevents the cilia from being able to remove the mucus, tar and dirt from the lungs, which leads to a 'smoker's cough' as the body tries to cough up mucus. Excess coughing can damage the alveoli and cause emphysema.

This smoking machine experiment (alongside) shows that cigarettes contain **tar**. Cigarettes also contain **nicotine,** which is very addictive, and produce **carbon monoxide** and particulates when they are burned. The carbon monoxide produced by a burning cigarette is dangerous because the blood picks it up instead of picking up oxygen. This means the blood is carrying much less oxygen. This leaves smokers feeling breathless and can lead to heart disease.

Tar contains chemicals that are **irritants** and **carcinogens** (cancer-causing chemicals). **Particulates** in cigarette smoke accumulate in living tissue, e.g. lung tissue which can cause cancer.

It's currently illegal to smoke in enclosed public places in the UK. Do you agree with this?

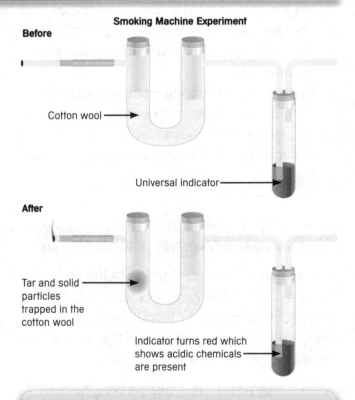

Smoking Machine Experiment

Before

Cotton wool

Universal indicator

After

Tar and solid particles trapped in the cotton wool

Indicator turns red which shows acidic chemicals are present

Quick Test

1. List two short-term effects of drinking alcohol.
2. What colour does the indicator change to on the smoking machine and why?
3. What part of cigarette smoke is carcinogenic?

Homeostasis

Your body has automatic control systems to maintain a constant internal environment to ensure that cells can function efficiently. This is called **homeostasis**. It is the maintenance of a constant internal environment.

Your body **balances** inputs and outputs to keep the internal environment steady, e.g. steady temperature, steady water levels and steady carbon dioxide levels in the blood.

Temperature Control

Enzymes in your body work best at **37°C**, so it's essential that your body remains very close to this temperature. Heat produced through respiration is used to maintain your body temperature.

If body temperature becomes too **high**, blood vessels widen and the blood flows closer to the skin so heat can be transferred to the environment. This is also done by sweating – the evaporation of sweat requires heat energy to be removed from the skin.

Getting too hot can be very dangerous. If too much water is lost through sweating, the body becomes **dehydrated**. This can lead to **heat stroke** and even **death**.

If the body temperature falls too **low**, blood vessels constrict and the blood flow near the skin is reduced, sweating stops and muscles start making tiny contractions, commonly known as shivers. These contractions need energy from respiration, and heat is released as a by-product.

Getting too cold can be fatal. **Hypothermia** is when the body temperature drops below 35°C. This causes **unconsciousness** and sometimes **death**. Putting on more clothing and doing exercise can help to raise body temperature.

Body temperature readings can be taken from the mouth, ear, skin surface, finger or anus. Although an anal temperature reading is the most accurate, it's normally only used in hospitals. Digital recording probes and thermal imaging are also used in hospitals. At home, heat-sensitive strips that are placed on the forehead are an alternative to clinical **thermometers**, which go under the tongue.

HT Blood temperature is **monitored** by the **brain**, which switches various temperature control mechanisms on and off. Vasodilation and vasoconstriction are the widening and narrowing (respectively) of the blood vessels close to the skin's surface in order to increase or reduce heat loss by radiation.

Negative feedback involves the automatic reversal of a change in condition. It occurs frequently in homeostasis. For example, if the temperature falls too low, the brain switches on mechanisms to raise it. If the temperature then becomes too high, the brain switches on mechanisms to lower it.

Blood temperature is monitored by the brain using the nervous system and the hormonal system. Temperature control systems work to keep a constant temperature.

Vasodilation – When the Body is too Warm

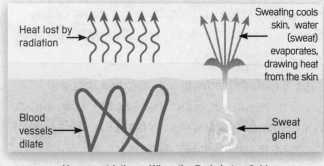

Vasoconstriction – When the Body is too Cold

B1 Staying in Balance

Hormones

Hormones are chemical messages released by **glands** directly into the bloodstream. They travel around the body to their target organs.

Hormones travel much **slower** (at the speed of blood) than a nervous impulse, which is an electrical message relayed directly to the target organs.

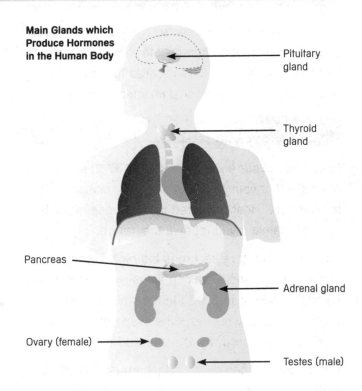

Main Glands which Produce Hormones in the Human Body

- Pituitary gland
- Thyroid gland
- Pancreas
- Adrenal gland
- Ovary (female)
- Testes (male)

Diabetes

The hormone **insulin** is released by the pancreas to control blood sugar levels. Insulin travels in the blood.

Type I diabetes is caused by the pancreas failing to produce **insulin**. This can lead to blood sugar levels rising fatally high and resulting in a **coma** or death. So blood sugar has to be controlled by injecting insulin into the blood.

Type II diabetes affects the cells that respond to insulin. They become desensitised to insulin and do not respond. Injecting insulin is no use. This type of diabetes is usually treated by diet.

(HT) Insulin helps to **regulate** a person's blood sugar levels by converting excess **glucose** in the blood to **glycogen** in the liver. People with diabetes might need to inject insulin before meals.

Before injecting insulin, a person with diabetes tests the amount of sugar in their blood with a prick test:
- If they have had food containing a lot of sugar then a bigger dose of insulin is required to reduce the blood sugar level.
- If they intend to exercise, then a smaller dose is required as they will use up a lot of sugar (for energy).

Quick Test

1. Give a brief definition of homeostasis.
2. What causes type I diabetes?
3. How does insulin travel around the body?
4. Are the body's reactions to hormones slower or faster than nervous reaction?

Hormone • Insulin • Diabetes

Plant Hormones

Plants, as well as animals, respond to changes in the environment. Plant **hormones** are chemicals that control:

- the growth of shoots and roots
- flowering and the ripening of fruits.

One group of plant hormones called **auxins** move through the plant in solution. They affect the plant's growth by responding to **gravity** (**geotropism**) and **light** (**phototropism**).

Shoots grow:
- towards light (positive phototropism)
- against gravity (negative geotropism).

Roots grow:
- away from light (negative phototropism)
- downwards in the direction of gravity (positive geotropism) to absorb water and provide support for the plant.

(HT) **Auxin** is made in the shoot **tip**. Its distribution through the plant is determined by light and can, therefore, be unequal. This is what happens when light shines on a shoot:

1. The hormones in direct sunlight are destroyed.
2. The hormones on the shaded side continue to function, causing the cells to elongate (lengthen).
3. The shoot bends towards the light.

Experiment to Show that Shoots Grow Towards Light

1. Cut a hole in the side of a box. Put three cuttings into the box. The cuttings detect light coming from the hole, and will grow towards it.

2. Cut a hole in the side of another box. Put three cuttings with foil-covered tips in the box. These shoots can't detect the light so they grow straight up.

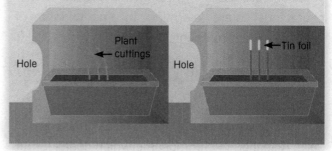

Growth towards light increases the plant's chance of survival as it can get light for photosynthesis.

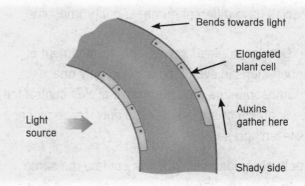

Commercial Uses of Hormones

Plant hormones can be used in agriculture to speed up or slow down plant growth. They include:

- **Rooting powder** – a hormone which encourages the growth of roots in stem cuttings, so many plants can be obtained from one plant.
- **Fruit-ripening hormone** – causes fruit to ripen. Ripening can be accelerated or delayed if required for transportation or storage.
- **Control of dormancy** – hormones can be used to speed up or slow down plant growth and bud development.

- **Selective weedkillers** – hormones in the weedkiller disrupt the growth patterns of their target plants without harming other plants. The broad leaved weeds have a larger surface area than the crop plants with narrow leaves so they receive a bigger dose of hormones and die.

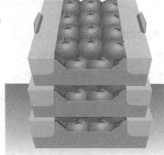

B1 Variation and Inheritance

Variation

Differences between individuals of the same species are **variations**. **Genetic** variations occur because individuals **inherit** different combinations of genes. They can be caused by mutations (changes to the genes), differences between individual **gametes** (i.e. eggs and sperm) or the random nature of fertilisation.

Individuals develop in different **conditions**, so some variations are due to **environmental** causes. Some characteristics are determined by a **combination** of genetic and environmental factors.

Genetic	Environmental	Combination
• Nose shape • Eye colour	• Language • Scars	• Body mass • Intelligence • Height

(HT) Scientists are currently debating whether genetics or environment has the greatest influence in the development of characteristics like intelligence, health and sporting ability. It's unlikely that any characteristics are the sole result of one factor.

Alleles

All the instructions to make an individual are held on **chromosomes** kept in the nucleus of all body cells. A section of chromosome which codes for an inherited characteristic or protein is called a **gene**. A person has 23 pairs of chromosomes; different species have different numbers of chromosome pairs. **Gametes** have half the number of chromosomes of normal body cells.

The different versions of genes are called **alleles**. Alleles that control characteristics are described as being **dominant** or **recessive**.

(HT) **Dominant** alleles control the development of a characteristic even if present on **only one** chromosome in a pair. **Recessive** alleles control the development of a characteristic only if a dominant allele isn't present.

If both chromosomes in a pair contain the **same allele** of a gene, the person is described as being **homozygous** for that gene or condition. If the chromosomes in a pair contain **different alleles**, the person is **heterozygous** for that gene or condition.

When a **characteristic** is **determined** by just **one** pair of alleles, as with eye colour and tongue rolling, it's called **monohybrid inheritance**.

Genetic diagrams are used to show all combinations of alleles and outcomes for a particular gene:
- Capital letters are used for dominant alleles.
- Lower case letters are used for recessive alleles.

For example, for eye colour:
- brown is dominant, so a brown allele is 'B'
- blue is recessive so a blue allele is 'b'.

The letters to describe the genetic make-up are called the **genotype** (e.g. BB) The characteristic expressed is called the **phenotype** (e.g. brown eyes).

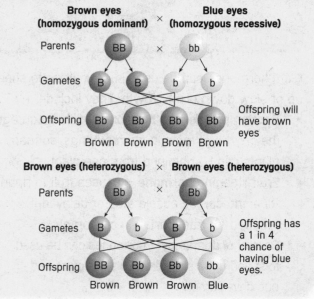

Inheritance of Sex

Gender (in mammals) is determined by the **sex chromosomes**: XX = female; XY = male.
Egg cells all carry X chromosomes. Half of **sperm cells** carry X chromosomes and half carry Y chromosomes.

The sex of an individual depends on whether the egg is **fertilised** by an X- or Y-carrying sperm:

*   An egg fertilised by an X sperm will become a girl (X from egg and X from sperm = XX).
*   An egg fertilised by a Y sperm will become a boy (X from egg and Y from sperm = XY).

The **chances** of an egg being fertilised by an X-carrying sperm or a Y-carrying sperm are equal, so there are approximately equal numbers of male and female offspring.

(HT) This genetic diagram shows a 50 : 50 chance of having a boy or girl:

		Male	
		X	Y
Female	X	X X	X Y
	X	X X	X Y

Inherited Diseases

Some diseases are caused by a 'faulty' gene, which means they can be **inherited**. Examples include red–green colour blindness, sickle cell anaemia and cystic fibrosis.

Knowing that there is an inherited disease in a family raises issues, e.g. whether to have children or not, whether to abort an affected foetus.

(HT) Inherited disorders such as cystic fibrosis are mostly caused by **recessive faulty alleles**. The gene for cystic fibrosis is **recessive**, which means that offspring will only have the disorder if **both** genes are faulty.

This genetic diagram (alongside) shows how the cystic fibrosis gene can be passed on to offspring from two **healthy** parents. (The parents don't have the disease because their dominant genes **protect** them.) It shows that there is a 1 in 4 chance that a child will have cystic fibrosis if both its parents are carriers.

Knowing the likelihood that their child could have cystic fibrosis means parents can make decisions about whether to have a child. But this is a very difficult decision.

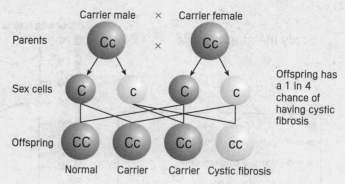

Quick Test

1. What are auxins?
2. Which are the female sex chromosomes – XX or XY?
3. What causes conditions like cystic fibrosis?

1 Louise regularly goes out drinking at the weekends. Explain the short-term effects that the alcohol could have on Louise's body. **[4]**

_____

_____

_____

2 Naveed feels ill and thinks he has a temperature. He thinks his friend at school has given him the flu.

a) Describe how Naveed could measure his body temperature. **[1]**

_____

b) Naveed has a body temperature of 39°C. Could he be ill? Explain your answer. **[2]**

_____

c) In what way does the body prevent microorganisms getting into the lungs? Put a tick (✓) in the box next to the correct answer.

Hydrochloric acid is made ☐　　　Tears are made ☐　　　Mucus is made ☐ **[1]**

d) What type of microorganism has caused Naveed's flu? **[1]**

_____

3 **a)** In mammals, gender is determined by sex chromosomes. Which of the following results in a female? Ring the correct answer.

XY　　　　XX　　　　YY　　　　XYY　　　　YXY **[1]**

b) What are different versions of genes called? **[1]**

_____

4 Study the graph below.

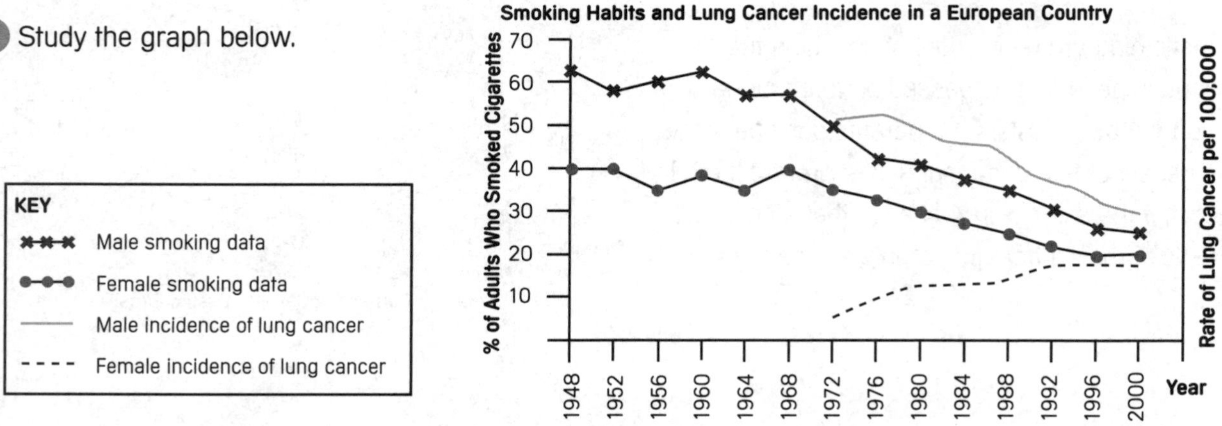

Smoking Habits and Lung Cancer Incidence in a European Country

KEY
✖✖✖ Male smoking data
●●● Female smoking data
— Male incidence of lung cancer
– – – Female incidence of lung cancer

% of Adults Who Smoked Cigarettes

Rate of Lung Cancer per 100,000

Year: 1948, 1952, 1956, 1960, 1964, 1968, 1972, 1976, 1980, 1984, 1988, 1992, 1996, 2000

a) Describe the pattern of smoking habits since 1972. **[2]**

_____

b) What differences are there in male and female cancer rates? **[2]**

_____

5 This newspaper article gives some information about a new drug.

> **Dieters' dream drug – The Fat Fighter?**
>
> A new drug known as 'ULose' has just been developed that might help people lose weight.
>
> Doctors say that about 11 million people in Britain are obese.
>
> The new drug works by stopping neurotransmitters passing messages between neurones in the brain. This stops people feeling hungry.
>
> Synapses in the brain are affected. Scientists also believe that this drug can help people give up smoking.

a) The new drug may help people to give up smoking. Why is it so hard for people to give up smoking? **[1]**

b) Delroy thinks he might be obese. His body mass is 100 kg and his height is 1.7 metres.

Use this formula to work out if Delroy is obese: $BMI = \dfrac{Mass\ in\ kg}{(Height\ in\ m)^2}$ **[3]**

BMI = ... Is Delroy obese? ....

Explanation: ....

c) Would Delroy benefit from the new drug? .... **[1]**

d) Another new drug called 'LJ3' has been developed to help people lose weight. Clinical trials are carried out on ULose and LJ3. The results are shown in the table.

Drug	Number of Volunteers in Trial	Average Weight Loss in 6 Weeks (kg)
LJ3	3250	3.2
ULose	700	5.8
Placebo	2800	2.6

i) In which trial would the data be most reliable? Explain your answer. **[2]**

ii) What conclusion could you draw from the data? **[2]**

iii) Why was a placebo given to some volunteers? **[2]**

HT e) The scientists think that the new drug 'ULose' works because its molecules are similar in shape to the neurotransmitter molecule. Suggest why this stops the passing of messages. **[2]**

6 Ben is running a 10 kilometre race this afternoon. For lunch he decides to have an omelette made of three eggs as he thinks this will provide energy for him in the race later on. Explain whether Ben is correct. **[1]**

B2 Classification

Classification Systems

Classification systems change over time. All living things used to be lumped together into two **kingdoms**: plants and animals. There are now five kingdoms. Living organisms are classified (grouped) according to shared **characteristics**. The five kingdoms are shown in the table.

Kingdom	Features	Feeding Method	Movement
Protista / Protoctista	Single-celled, have a nucleus, some have some chloroplasts, no cell wall, organelles present	Photosynthesis or ingestion of other organisms or both.	Move using cilia or flagella.
Monera (Prokaryotes)	Single-celled, no nucleus, no chloroplasts, have a cell wall	Absorb nutrients through cell wall, or produce their own.	May or may not move.
Fungi	Multicellular, have a nucleus, no chloroplasts, have a cell wall	Acquire nutrients from decaying material.	No mechanisms for movement.
Plants	Multicellular, have a nucleus, chloroplasts and cell walls	Require sunlight to make food through photosynthesis.	Most don't move.
Animals	Multicellular, have a nucleus, no chloroplasts, no cell walls	Acquire nutrients by ingestion.	Move using cilia, flagella or muscles.

(HT) This classification system may need to be changed in the future as more **species** are found and new discoveries, especially in genetics, are made. Accepted systems of classification have historically changed.

Problems Classifying Organisms

Some organisms from different species can mate and reproduce to give birth to a hybrid. Hybrids aren't fertile so they can't be called a new species.

Classifying some organisms, e.g. those in a micro-environment, can be difficult. The variety of life is a continuous spectrum which makes it difficult to place some organisms into distinct groups. Organisms that only reproduce asexually can be hard to classify. Organisms are constantly changing to suit their environment.

Evolutionary Trees

Evolutionary relationships between organisms in the kingdoms can be displayed in **evolutionary trees**.

Monera represent the earliest group of organisms. Monera gave rise to Protista, from which the three other kingdoms of organisms evolved along separate lines. This is a theory that not all scientists agree on.

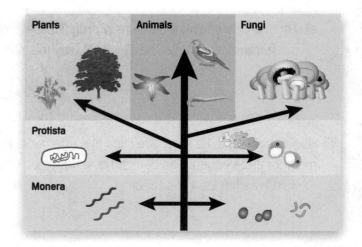

Characteristics • Protista • Fungi • Hybrid

Species

The five kingdoms are divided into **phyla**. Each phylum is divided into **classes**; each class into **orders**; each order into **families**; each family into **genera**; each genus into **species**.

Members of the same species can reproduce together to produce fertile offspring, but within a species there is still lots of variation. Each species is given two Latin names, e.g. *Homo sapiens*: this is the **binomial naming system**. Members of a species have more features in common than they do with other organisms of a different species and so tend to live in the same habitat. But, closely related species can be found on different continents where conditions are different so the species may have evolved over time to adapt to the different conditions. Species inherit characteristics so we expect similar species to be closely related to a **common ancestor**.

Species classification takes into account evolutionary relationships as well as ecological relationships.

HT Not all organisms with similar characteristics are descended from a common ancestor. They may have evolved to survive in the same environment so developed similar structures.

For example, whales, dolphins and sharks look quite similar but they're developed from different ancestors. Their similarities are due to sharing a similar environment for millions of years.

HT Artificial and Natural Classification

Artificial classification is based on observed characteristics, e.g. beaks, and is designed for a practical purpose, convenience and simplicity, e.g. **Linnaeus** included all worm-like organisms in a single group; the group included simple nematodes as well as snakes.

Natural classification tries to use natural relationships between organisms. It considers more evidence, including internal and external features. Most classifications today are natural and based on evolutionary relationships.

DNA sequencing has helped with understanding classification. Organisms that are closely related, e.g. brown bears and polar bears have a high degree of DNA sequence similarity.

Arthropods

Invertebrates can be divided into different groups, one of which is the **arthropods**, the largest animal group. Arthropods have limbs with joints that allow them to move, and an exoskeleton, which is shed as they grow. Arthropods are divided into four classes as shown in the table:

Arthropod	Features	Examples
Crustacean	10 or more legs, antennae	Crabs, lobsters
Insect	6 legs, antennae	Dragonflies
Arachnid	8 legs, no antennae	Spiders, mites, scorpions
Myriapod	8–750 legs, antennae	Centipedes, millipedes

B2 Energy Flow

Food Chains

Food chains show the **transfer of energy** from organism to organism. Energy from the Sun flows through a food chain when green plants absorb sunlight to make glucose, and through feeding. Green plants are producers because they produce biomass during photosynthesis (Algae and plankton are other examples of producers). Consumers are organisms which eat other organisms. All other organisms in food chains rely on plants.

In ecology, the **trophic level** is the position or stage that an organism occupies in a food chain, what it eats and what eats it.

Biomass and energy are lost at every trophic level of a food chain. Materials and energy are lost in an organism's faeces during egestion. Energy is lost through **movement** and **respiration**, especially in birds and mammals, through heat loss and waste (excretion) and so it doesn't go into making new biomass.

Excretory products and uneaten parts can be used as the starting point for other food chains, e.g. dung beetles eating elephant faeces.

Organisms which eat both plants and animals can be both primary and secondary consumers, e.g. humans.

A Food Chain

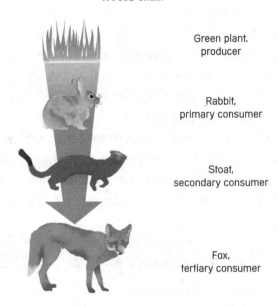

Green plant, producer

Rabbit, primary consumer

Stoat, secondary consumer

Fox, tertiary consumer

Efficiency of Energy Transfer

The length of a food chain depends on the **efficiency of energy transfer**. In the food chain above:

- A fraction of the Sun's energy is captured by the producers.
- The rabbits respire and produce waste products. They pass on a tenth of the energy they get from the grass (10%); 90% is lost.
- The stoats respire and produce waste products. They pass on a tenth of the energy they get from the rabbits (10%); 90% is lost.
- The fox gets the last tiny bit of energy left after all the others have had a share.

Food chains rarely have fourth or fifth degree consumers as there isn't enough energy to pass on.

If you know how much energy is stored in the living organisms at each level of a food chain, you can calculate the efficiency of energy transfer:

$$\text{Energy efficiency} = \frac{\text{Energy converted to biomass}}{\text{Total energy taken in}} \times 100$$

Example

A sheep eats 100kJ of energy in the form of grass, but only 9kJ becomes new sheep tissue. The rest is lost as faeces, urine or heat. Calculate the efficiency of energy transfer in the sheep.

$$\text{Energy efficiency} = \frac{9}{100} \times 100 = \textbf{9\%}$$

  Producers • Biomass • Photosynthesis • Consumer • Egestion

Food Webs

Food chains link up to make **food webs**. If organisms are removed from, or added to, a food web it has a huge impact on all the other organisms. For example, if the seaweed was removed from this food web, the fish and the winkle numbers may go down due to less food. This may then cause seal and lobster numbers to go down.

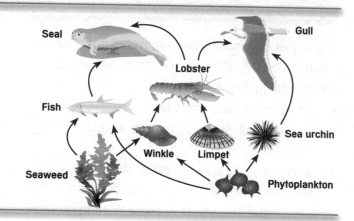

Pyramids of Numbers

The number of organisms at each stage in a food chain can be shown as a **pyramid of numbers**.

The number of organisms decreases as you go up the pyramid, i.e. a lot of grass feeds a few rabbits, which feed even fewer stoats, which feed just one fox.

For simplicity, pyramids of numbers usually look like this:

Pyramids of numbers don't take into account the **mass** of the organisms, so it's possible to end up with some odd-looking pyramids. For example, if lots of slugs feed on one lettuce, the base of the

pyramid is smaller than the next stage. This happens because the lettuce is a large organism compared to the slug. This situation also happens when trees are at the bottom of a food chain.

(HT) There are problems with creating pyramids of numbers. Some organisms may belong to more than one trophic level and measuring biomass is tricky as it involves drying out and weighing the mass of an organism, which isn't easy with large organisms like trees.

Pyramids of Biomass

Pyramids of biomass show the dry mass of living material at each stage in the chain. They're always pyramid shaped because they take the **mass** of the organisms into account.

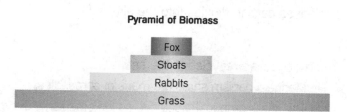

Pyramid of Biomass

Quick Test

1 What is a trophic level?
2 Name the four arthropod classes.
3 List the four ways in which energy is lost at each stage of a food chain.
4 (HT) Why is it difficult to classify hybrids?

(HT) The efficiency of energy transfer **explains the shape of biomass pyramids**. Biomass is lost through the stages. A lot of biomass remains in the ground as the root system. The rabbits and stoats lose biomass in faeces and urine. The fox gets the remaining biomass.

B2 Recycling

Recycling

In a stable community, the removal of materials is balanced by the return of materials. So materials are constantly being recycled:

- When animals and plants **grow**, they **take in** elements from the soil which are incorporated into their bodies.
- When animals **die** and **decay**, these mineral elements are **released** and can be taken up by other living organisms to allow them to grow.

Carbon and **nitrogen** are two recycled elements.

In waterlogged or acidic soils, the recycling of nutrients takes longer. This is because waterlogged soil lacks oxygen for decomposers and acidic soil is not the best pH for decomposers.

The Carbon Cycle

The constant recycling of carbon is called the **carbon cycle**.

1. Carbon dioxide is removed from the atmosphere by green plants for photosynthesis.
2. Plants and animals respire, releasing carbon dioxide into the atmosphere.
3. Soil, bacteria and fungi (**decomposers**) feed on dead plants and animals, causing them to break down, decay and release carbon dioxide into the air. (The **microorganisms** respire as they feed, passing carbon compounds along the food chain.) This decay process makes elements available again to living organisms.

Feeding passes carbon compounds along a food chain. The burning of fossil fuels (combustion) also releases carbon dioxide into the air.

Soil bacteria and fungi are decomposers. They feed on dead animals and plants and then respire, releasing carbon dioxide into the air.

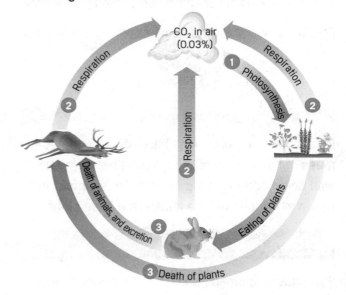

Carbon is also recycled in the sea.

1. Marine organism shells are made of carbonates. The shells drop to the sea bed as the organisms die.
2. The shells fossilise to become limestone rock.
3. Volcanic eruptions heat the limestone and release carbon dioxide into the atmosphere. Carbon dioxide is also released during weathering of the limestone rock.
4. Oceans absorbing carbon dioxide act as **carbon sinks**.

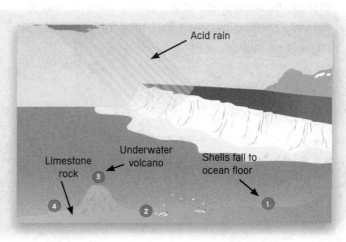

Decay • Decomposers • Microorganism

The Nitrogen Cycle

The air is made up of approximately 78% **nitrogen**. Nitrogen is a vital element used in the production of **proteins**, which are needed for growth in plants and animals. A lot of nitrogen is stored in the air, but animals and plants can't use it because it's so **unreactive**.

The **nitrogen cycle** shows how nitrogen and its compounds are recycled in nature:

1. Plants absorb **nitrates** from the soil to make protein for growth.
2. Animals eat plants and use the nitrogen to make animal protein. Feeding passes nitrogen compounds along a food chain.
3. Dead animals and plants are broken down by decomposers, releasing nitrates back into the soil.

HT The Role of Bacteria

Nitrogen-fixing bacteria convert atmospheric nitrogen into nitrates in the soil. Some of these bacteria live in the soil while others live in root nodules with certain plants (legumes), e.g. peas and beans.

Nitrifying bacteria convert ammonium compounds into nitrates in the soil.

Denitrifying bacteria convert nitrates and ammonium compounds into atmospheric nitrogen.

The energy released by lightning causes oxygen and nitrogen in the air to combine to form nitrogen oxides which dissolve in water. Soil bacteria and fungi act as decomposers, converting proteins and urea into ammonia.

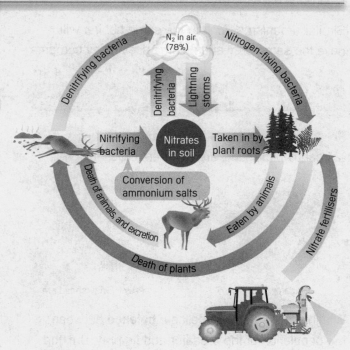

Quick Test

1. Name two recycled elements.
2. How much nitrogen is found naturally in the air?
3. HT Describe the function of nitrifying bacteria.

B2 Interdependence

Competing for Resources

The size and distribution of any **population** of plants or animals will change over time. It can be affected by how well the organisms **compete** for **limited resources**. Similar animals in the same habitat will be in close competition.

Animals compete for food, water, shelter and mates. **Plants** compete for light, water and minerals.

(HT) There are two types of competition: **interspecific** and **intraspecific**. Interspecific competition is where individuals of different species compete for the same resources in an ecosystem, e.g. food or space. Intraspecific competition is where individuals from the same species are competing for the same resource. Intraspecific competition is more significant as these organisms have the exact same needs.

Similar organisms living in the same habitat will have the same prey and nesting sites. They compete

The **better-adapted** competitors will get most of the resources, so they can **survive** and **produce** offspring.

The **interdependence** of organisms determines their distribution and abundance.

to occupy the same **ecological niche** (place and function). They will be in direct competition for the resources they need. For example:

- different ladybird species
- red and grey squirrels.

Red squirrels are the native species to the UK. Grey squirrels were introduced from the USA in 1876, forcing both squirrel species to compete for the same resources. This has led to red squirrels becoming an **endangered** species.

Cycles of Predators and Prey

Predators are animals that kill and eat other animals. Animals that are eaten are called the **prey**.

Predator – Lynx   **Prey** – Snowshoe hare

Within nature there's a delicate **balance** between the population of the predator and its prey. But, the prey will always **outnumber** the predators.

There will be **cyclical fluctuations** in the numbers of each species because the numbers of predator and prey will **regulate** each other.

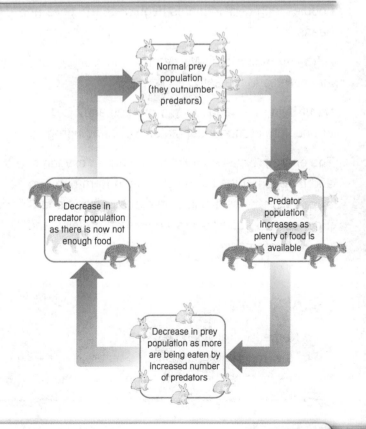

Normal prey population (they outnumber predators)

Predator population increases as plenty of food is available

Decrease in prey population as more are being eaten by increased number of predators

Decrease in predator population as there is now not enough food

HT Cycles of Predators and Prey (Cont.)

When there are lots of hares the lynx have more food so they breed and their numbers go up.

But they then eat lots of hares, so lynx numbers go down. With less food available, the fox numbers go down. Because it is cause and effect, the peaks and troughs in predator and prey numbers are out of phase.

Parasitic Relationships

Some organisms survive by living off other organisms. They are known as **parasites**, e.g. fleas, tapeworms. The organism they live off is known as the **host** organism.

Parasites can make the host organism ill or even kill it. For example, **tapeworms** (parasites) can be contracted by humans (hosts) by eating pork infected with tapeworm larvae (also known as bladderworms). The tapeworm absorbs food from the person's gut. This can make them very ill.

Flea – a Parasite

Mutualistic Relationships

In **mutualistic** relationships, two organisms form a relationship from which both organisms benefit.

For example, **oxpecker birds** live on **buffalos'** backs.

The oxpecker gets a ready supply of food from the flies and ticks on a buffalo's skin.

The buffalo also benefits as the birds get rid of the pests and provide an early warning system by hissing when lions or other predators approach.

Organisms performing this function, such as oxpecker birds, are known as 'cleaner' species.

Buffalo and Oxpecker Bird – Mutualistic Relationship

HT Another example of a mutualistic relationship can be found in **leguminous plants**, e.g. the pea plant. **Bacteria** in the root nodules take sugars from the plant to use in respiration. They also convert nitrogen into nitrates, which benefits the plant because it enables it to survive in nitrogen-poor soils. So the bacteria gain sugars and the plant gains nitrates.

Quick Test

1. **a)** What is the term given to organisms that survive by living off other organisms?
   b) Give an example of a mutualistic relationship.
2. HT Name the type of competition which takes place between members of the same species.

B2 Adaptations

Adaptations

Adaptations are special **features** or **behaviours** that make an organism particularly well **suited** to its **environment**. As plants and animals become better adapted to their environment, they become better able to **compete** for limited **resources**, which enables their **population size** and **distribution** (where they are found) to increase.

If climate changes, those organisms that can successfully adapt to the new conditions will survive.

Adaptations to Cold Environments

Adaptations to very cold environments help organisms to survive. Examples include:

- being well insulated to reduce heat loss
- having a small surface area to volume ratio to prevent heat loss
- behavioural adaptations to help animals to survive cold temperatures, e.g. hedgehogs and groundhogs **hibernate** in winter and birds **migrate** to warmer climates.

The **polar bear** has several adaptations to allow it to survive in a very cold climate:

- Small ears and large bulk reduce surface area to volume ratio to reduce heat loss.
- Large amount of insulating blubber beneath the skin.
- Thick white fur for insulation and camouflage.
- Large feet to spread its weight on snow and ice.
- Fur on the soles of its paws give insulation and grip.
- Powerful legs for running and swimming.

Counter-current Heat Exchange Systems

Penguins have a **heat exchange blood flow** to the colder regions. Warm blood entering the feet and flippers flows past cold blood leaving the feet and flippers and warms it up. The warmed up blood re-enters the rest of the body and doesn't affect the penguin's core temperature.

Adaptations to Hot and Dry Environments

Animals in hot environments have behavioural methods of coping with the heat, e.g. finding somewhere cool to go, only going out at night and shedding fur, which all reduce heat gain. Behaviours like taking a swim and panting increase heat loss.

Cacti cope with a lack of water by having long roots to reach water, a thick waxy cuticle to reduce water loss and having spines to reduce water loss and protect water stored in the spongy layer from predators.

Adaptations to Hot and Dry Environments (Cont.)

Camels have several adaptations to allow them to survive in a very hot climate:

- Body fat stored in hump so there's very little insulation under the skin, which keeps it cooler.
- Drinks many litres of water in one go and stores the extra water in the blood.
- Able to tolerate changes in body temperature so doesn't need to sweat very much.

- Hair-lined nostrils trap moisture in its breath before it's exhaled, and the moisture is returned to the body.

Other organisms are also able to trap moisture, for example, desert rats have a long snout-like nose which means they're able to trap moisture to return to the body.

Extremophiles

Some organisms are biochemically adapted to extreme conditions. These organisms are called extremophiles. They have enzymes that work at different optimum conditions, e.g. bacteria that live in thermal vents. Some organisms that live in very cold conditions, e.g. some Antarctic fish, possess **anti-freeze proteins** (AFPs) to prevent ice crystals growing inside tissues.

Specialists and Generalists

Some organisms are specialists so are only suited to certain habitats. Other organisms are generalists so they can live in a range of habitats, but can be easily out-competed by other organisms.

Predator and Prey Adaptations

Animals have adapted depending on their position in the food chain, i.e. whether they are predators (and have to chase prey) or prey (who need to escape from predators).

Predators, e.g. lions, polar bears, usually:
- are built for bursts of speed
- are camouflaged to avoid being spotted
- have sharp teeth and claws to grab and kill prey
- have eyes at the front of their head, which provides three-dimensional vision and accurate perception of size and distance (binocular vision)
- have a hunting strategy
- have fewer young than prey animals and give them more care so they survive to adulthood.

Prey, e.g. rabbits, deer, usually:
- are built for speed so they can escape quickly
- are well-camouflaged in their environment – they have cryptic or warning colouration
- live in groups, to increase the opportunities for detecting and confusing predators
- have eyes positioned on the sides of their head for a wide field of view so that they can see predators approaching
- use breeding strategies like synchronous breeding and have more young than predator animals as many get eaten
- use **mimicry** to protect themselves from predators, e.g. the coral snake's banded pattern is copied by harmless snakes to ward off predators.

B2 Natural Selection

The Theory of Evolution

Animals and plants that are better adapted to their environment are more likely to survive. This theory is called natural selection and was first put forward by **Charles Darwin**.

Evolution is the slow, continual **change** of organisms over a very long period to become better **adapted** to their environment. These changes arise through **mutations** (changes in DNA).

These adaptations are controlled by genes and can be **passed on** to future generations.

If the environment changes, species must change with it if they are to survive. Animals and plants that are better adapted to their environment are more likely to survive. This is called **natural selection**. Species that aren't well-adapted to their environment may become extinct.

Examples of Natural Selection Today

Peppered Moths

Peppered moths can be pale or dark. Pale peppered moths are easily camouflaged amongst the lichens on silver birch tree bark.

But, in areas of high pollution, the bark on silver birch trees is discoloured by soot. In these areas, the rarer, darker speckled varieties of the peppered moth are more common than the pale varieties. This is because the pale peppered moths show up against the sooty bark, whereas the darker peppered moths are camouflaged. So, they're able to survive and breed in greater numbers.

Bacteria and Penicillin

Some **bacteria** have become **resistant** to penicillin by natural selection, as follows:

1 Bacteria mutated. Some were resistant to the antibiotic penicillin; others were not.
2 The non-resistant bacteria were more likely to be killed by the penicillin.
3 The penicillin-resistant bacteria survived.
4 The surviving bacteria reproduce, leading to more bacteria that are resistant to penicillin.

This is why doctors are reluctant to prescribe antibiotics unless they're absolutely necessary.

Natural selection as a theory is now widely accepted.

It explains many observations in nature like the peppered moth. It has also been discussed and tested worldwide by many scientists.

Although the theory of natural selection explains many observations, it doesn't prove that the explanation is correct.

Dark Peppered Moth

Peppered Moth

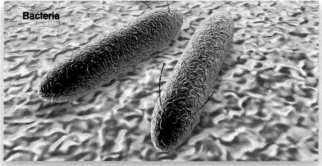

Bacteria

Natural selection • Gene • Extinct

Lamarck's Theory

Lamarck suggested that evolution happened by the **inheritance of acquired characteristics**:

1. Organisms change **during their lifetime** as they struggle to survive.
2. These changes are passed on to their offspring.

Lamarck's theory was **rejected** because there was no evidence that the changes that happened in an individual's lifetime could alter their genes and so be passed on to their offspring. This theory was very different from Darwin's theory and had no genetic basis.

Evolution by Natural Selection

After making extensive observations, **Charles Darwin** proposed his theory of **Evolution by Natural Selection**.

Evolution is the **specialisation** of a population over many generations to become better **adapted** to its environment. There are four key points to remember:

1. Individuals within a population show **natural variation** (i.e. differences due to their genes).
2. There is **competition** between individuals for limited resources (e.g. food, mates) and also predation and disease, which keep population sizes constant in spite of the production of many offspring, i.e. there is a 'struggle for survival', and weaker individuals die.
3. Individuals that are **better adapted** to the environment are more likely to **survive**, breed successfully and produce offspring. This is termed **'survival of the fittest'**.
4. These survivors will therefore pass on their 'successful' **genes** to their **offspring**, resulting in an improved organism being evolved through natural selection.

Species which are unable to compete become **extinct**.

Groups of the same species who are separated from each other by physical boundaries like mountains or seas will not be able to breed and share their genes. This is because over long periods of time, the separate groups may specialise so much that they can't successfully breed any longer and so two new species are formed.

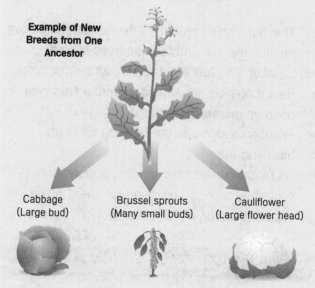

Example of New Breeds from One Ancestor

Cabbage (Large bud)　　Brussel sprouts (Many small buds)　　Cauliflower (Large flower head)

As new discoveries have been made, and a better understanding of genetics and inheritance is known, the theory of natural selection has been developed and updated.

Many theories have been put forward to explain how evolution may occur. The theory of evolution by natural selection was initially met with hostility. Darwin's ideas went against those of the Church and the Bible. Most scientists now accept the theory put forward by Darwin, but there is still debate amongst some scientists.

Quick Test

1. Who first put forward the theory of evolution?
2. Explain why a species might become extinct or endangered.
3. What organism shows natural selection in action today?
4. Why were Darwin's ideas not popular?

B2 Population and Pollution

Pollution

The human population is increasing at a rapid rate. This is the result of the birth rate exceeding the death rate.

This increase in population results in an increase in the demand for **finite** resources, like **fossil fuels** and minerals, which are used for fuel.

As more fossil fuels and oils are burned to produce energy, a greater amount of **pollution** is produced, in particular:

- household waste and sewage
- sulfur dioxide and carbon dioxide.

Pollution can affect the number and type of organisms that can survive. For example, dark peppered moths will survive in polluted areas; pale ones will be eaten as they aren't camouflaged.

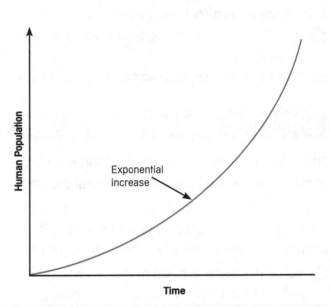

Increase in Human Population

Human Population / Time

Exponential increase

(HT) The exponential growth of the human population means that the demand for resources is also exponential. This has a number of consequences:

- Raw materials like oil and minerals are being used up increasingly quickly.
- Pollution and waste are building up at an alarming rate.
- As resources become in short supply there is more and more competition for basic things like food and water, which become more expensive.

Although the **developed countries** of the world (e.g. USA, UK, France and Japan) have only a small proportion of the world's population, they use the greatest amount of resources and produce the largest proportion of pollution.

Carbon footprint is the term used to refer to the amount of greenhouse gases a person or event is responsible for emitting in a given timescale. The amount will depend on the person's lifestyle.

Ozone Depletion

Ozone is a **natural gas** found high up in the Earth's **atmosphere**.

It prevents too many harmful ultraviolet (UV) rays reaching the Earth.

Recently, scientists have noticed that the ozone layer is becoming thinner; it is **depleting**. Many people blame the use of **CFCs** (chlorofluorocarbons) in factories, fridges and aerosol cans for this change in the ozone layer. The consequence will be a rise in cases of skin cancer.

Acid Rain

Acid rain is caused by burning fossil fuels which release acid gases like sulfur dioxide and nitrogen oxides. These dissolve in rainwater to make acidic

rain. This leads to metals corroding, dissolving of rocks and statues, destruction of forests, and lakes becoming acidic, killing fish and other wildlife.

Fossil fuels • Pollution • Carbon footprint • Ozone

Global Warming

The atmosphere keeps the Earth warm; this is known as the **greenhouse effect**:

1. Heat energy from the Sun is reflected from the Earth's surface back out towards space.
2. When it reaches the atmosphere, some rays pass through, but others are trapped in by the carbon dioxide layer. These trapped rays keep the Earth warmer than it would be otherwise, and so allow life to exist.

The amount of carbon dioxide in the atmosphere has increased, which has led to more of the energy being **reflected** back. This is known as **global warming** because the Earth is gradually getting hotter. It may lead to the melting of the polar ice caps, flooding and changes in climate and weather patterns.

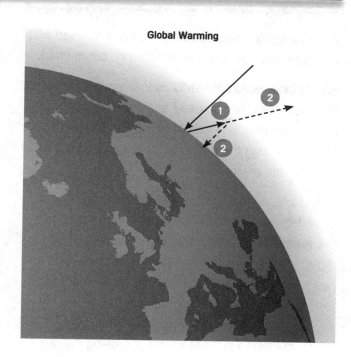

Global Warming

Living Organisms as Indicators

Pollution in the environment can drastically affect the **survival** of living organisms. Some organisms can only cope with 'clean' conditions; they are very sensitive to pollution, so they die. Other species have **evolved** to **resist** the **toxic** effects of pollution so they can **survive**. All these organisms are indicators of pollution and are called **indicator species**. For example, some varieties of lichens are able to survive when high levels of sulfur dioxide are present in the air. The presence of these varieties of lichens acts as an indicator of air pollution.

Some insect larvae, such as the rat-tailed maggot, the bloodworm, the waterlouse and the sludgeworm, can cope with high levels of nitrogen pumped into streams by sewage works outlets. The presence of these organisms is an indicator of water pollution.

Pollution can be measured by using indicator species or by directly measuring pollution levels.

HT

	Advantages	Disadvantages
Using living methods (indicator species)	Reliable, good indicators of long-term effects, easy to identify, cheap, has minimal impact on other organisms.	Seasonal variations, may be killed if pollution is too high, may become diseased and die, organisms may leave the area.
Using non-living methods	Can identify source of pollution, gives quantitative data which can be compared to other locations or time periods.	Expensive as special equipment and chemicals are needed, more people involved.

Quick Test

1. What does sulfur dioxide in the air cause?
2. How are indicator species useful?
3. HT Explain the term 'carbon footprint'.

B2 Sustainability

Sustainable Development

A **sustainable** **resource** is one that can be used and **replaced** so it isn't exhausted (used up completely).

Sustainable development is concerned with ensuring that resources can be used and maintained without compromising the needs of future generations. It's about providing the needs of the population without harming the environment.

Resources can be sustained whilst still being exploited by using **quotas** and ensuring resources are **replenished** or **restocked**, for example, replenishing and restocking pine forests by planting a new sapling for each mature tree cut down. Another example is **conserving** cod stocks:

- The mesh size of fishing nets has been increased to prevent young cod being caught before they reach breeding age.

- Cod quotas have been set to prevent over-fishing.
- Quotas of other fish have been increased.

Education is important so that local people understand the importance of conservation.

(HT) Exponential increase in human population size makes sustainable development quite a challenge. As the population increases rapidly, the demand for food and energy also increases. The quickest and cheapest ways to meet these demands aren't always the most sustainable.

Sustainability requires planning and **cooperation** at local, national and international levels. Sustainable development can help protect endangered species, e.g. quotas can be set for whaling.

Endangered Species

Endangered **species** are those that are in danger of becoming **extinct** unless something is done to prevent it. The panda and the gorilla are endangered species.

If the number of individuals or their habitats fall below a critical level, the organism is **critically endangered** which means they face an extremely high risk of extinction in the wild. Being critically endangered ranks above being endangered and is one step away from extinction.

The **survival** of plant or animal species can be threatened for a number of reasons, including:

- climate change
- destruction of habitats, e.g. by logging companies, which wipes out food sources and shelter
- hunting
- increased competition for food, shelter, etc.
- pollutants (from pollution) which can accumulate in marine mammals.

If endangered species aren't protected they could become extinct like the mammoth, the dodo and the sabre-toothed tiger. It is vitally important to conserve endangered species and habitats.

Endangered species can be **protected** by:
- **educating** people about sustainable development
- breeding animals in **captivity** (e.g. zoos) and possibly returning them to their natural habitat to create new populations
- **protecting** (conserving) natural **habitats**
- creating **artificial ecosystems** (e.g. zoos, aquariums) for the species to live in
- **legally protecting** endangered species, so they can't be trapped, killed or kept, except under special licence
- **prohibiting** the **hunting** of legally protected species
- making **seedbanks**.

(HT) If there isn't enough genetic variation in a population, species become at risk of extinction, e.g. if the organisms are genetically very similar, a disease that kills one may kill them all.

Conservation Programmes

Conservation programmes play an essential role in:

- protecting the human food supply by maintaining the genetic variety of crops, animals and plants
- stabilising ecosystems by ensuring minimal damage to food chains and habitats
- studying and identifying plants which might be useful to develop medicines to treat diseases
- protecting the culture of indigenous people living in threatened habitats such as the Amazonian rainforest.

Whales

Some whale species are now **endangered**, i.e. they are close to extinction. The main causes of whale deaths include:

- becoming entangled in fishing nets and drowning
- being affected by pollutants in the sea
- colliding with ships during migration
- effects of climate change affecting food sources
- culling and hunting.

Money can be made from whales whether they are dead or alive:

- Live whales can be a big tourist attraction.
- Dead whales can be used for food, oil and to make cosmetics.

Whales can be conserved by keeping them in captivity, and some zoos have had success with captive breeding. But, captive whales suffer loss of freedom by being reared in a zoo rather than their natural habitat. Often, whales are trained to perform or are used for research purposes.

(HT) There are many aspects of whale biology that we need to know more about, for example:

- how they communicate over large distances
- how they migrate
- how they dive and survive at extreme depths.

The International Whaling Commission makes **laws** to **protect** whale species and sets quotas for hunting. It's very difficult to enforce these laws though because it's impossible to police all the world's oceans.

It's also difficult to get all countries to agree. Many countries support the idea that whale hunting is unnecessary. But, some countries like Iceland, Norway and Japan disagree with a ban on killing whales. They feel it's necessary to preserve the fishing industry and carry out 'research culls' to investigate the effect of whale population size on fish stocks.

Quick Test

1. **a)** What is meant by the term 'endangered species'?
   b) How can we protect endangered species?
2. What are whales used for (dead and alive)?
3. **(HT)** Apart from making laws to protect whales, what does the International Whaling Commission do to protect whale numbers?

1 Amelia was listening to the news on the radio when she heard the following headline:

'Cod fishing needs to stop if we are to prevent stocks being virtually wiped out by 2050. However, the UK fisheries minister has ruled out a complete ban on cod fishing, saying that a "zero catch" would see "the end of all fishing in the UK".

a) The fishing industry can protect the cod through sustainable development. One way to sustain the cod is to set quotas. How does setting quotas help to protect the cod? **[1]**

b) It is possible that species like cod could become endangered or even extinct. Suggest two ways in which cod could become extinct, apart from as a result of fishing. **[2]**

2 Look at the picture of a polar bear.

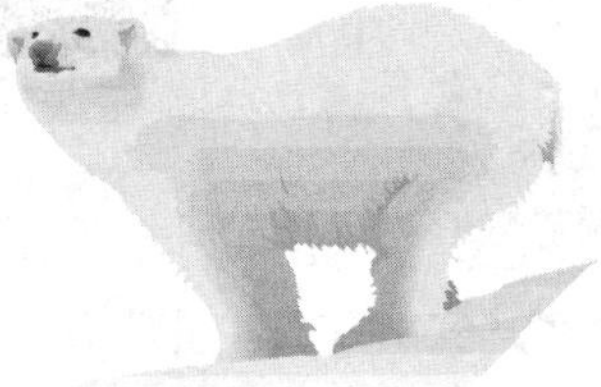

a) Describe and explain two modifications that polar bears have made to adapt to the cold conditions. **[4]**

b) If global warming leads to the melting of polar ice caps, how might this affect the polar bears and why? **[6]**

🖉 *The quality of written communication will be assessed in your answer to this question.*

3 Study each of the following organisms.

A   B 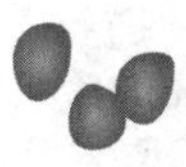   C 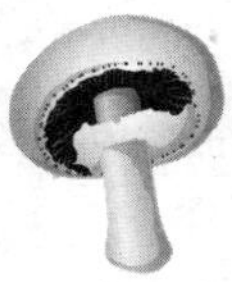   D 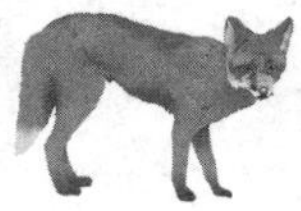   E

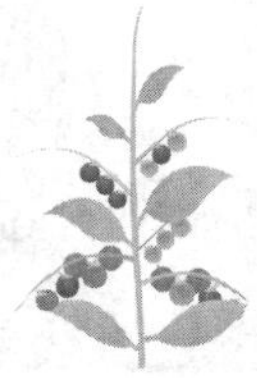

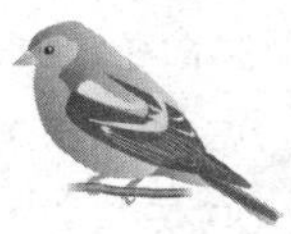

a) Which organism belongs to the fungus kingdom? Explain your answer. **[2]**

b) Which kingdom does organism **B** belong to? Give a reason for your answer. **[2]**

c) Another organism, **F**, moves using flagella. Which kingdom does it belong to? **[2]**

4 The table shows the classification of a number of species.

Kingdom	Phylum	Genus	Species	Common Name
Animal	Equidae	Equus	Zebra	Zebra
Animal	Equidae	Equus	Asinus	Donkey
Animal	Equidae	Equus	Ferus	Horse
Animal	Camelidae	Camelus	Ferus	Camel
Animal	Canidae	Canis	Lupus	Wolf

a) Write down the binomial name for a wolf. **[1]**

b) Suggest two species which are closely related. Explain your answer. **[2]**

5 Explain how a cactus is adapted to live in the desert. **[4]**

HT **6** The length of a food chain depends on the efficiency of energy transfer. Study the food chain below.

Grass ⟶ Grasshopper ⟶ Snake ⟶ Hawk
(70 000kJ)   (12 500kJ)   (2200kJ)   (120kJ)

a) Explain why this food chain does not have fourth or fifth degree consumers. **[1]**

b) The percentage energy transfer from producer to primary consumer is 17.9%. What is the percentage energy transfer from secondary consumer to tertiary consumer? **[2]**

Fundamental Chemical Concepts

You need to have a good understanding of the concepts (ideas) on these four pages, so make sure you revise this section before each exam.

Atoms

All substances are made up of **atoms**. Atoms have:
- a **positively** charged **nucleus** made of **protons** and **neutrons** (except hydrogen)
- **negatively** charged **electrons** that orbit the nucleus.

Atomic Particle	Relative Charge
Proton	+1
Neutron	0
Electron	-1

An atom contains the same number of electrons (negatively charged particles) and protons (positively charged particles), so each atom is electrically neutral. This means that it has no overall charge.

A Fluorine Atom

Key: ● Proton ● Neutron ✖ Electron

Elements and Compounds

An **element** is a substance made up of just one type of atom. Each element is represented by a different chemical symbol, for example:
- Fe represents iron
- Na represents sodium.

These symbols are all arranged in the **periodic table**.

Compounds are substances formed from the atoms of more than one element, which have been joined together by a chemical bond:
- **Covalent** bonds – two atoms **share** a pair of **electrons**. (The atoms in molecules are held together by covalent bonds.)
- **Ionic** bonds – atoms **lose electrons** to become **positive ions** or **gain electrons** to become **negative ions**. The attraction between oppositely charged ions is an **ionic bond**.

A Covalent Bond between Hydrogen and Carbon in Methane

Methane (CH_4)

An Ionic Bond between Sodium and Chlorine in Sodium Chloride

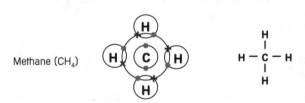

Sodium ion, Na^+ [2.8]$^+$

Chloride ion, Cl^- [2.8.8]$^-$

Key Words   Atom • Nucleus • Proton • Neutron • Electron • Element • Compound • Covalent • Ionic

Fundamental Chemical Concepts

Formulae

Chemical symbols are used with numbers to write **formulae** that represent compounds. Formulae are used to show:

- the different elements in a compound
- the number of atoms of each element in the formula.

If there are brackets around part of the formula, everything inside the brackets is multiplied by the number outside.

Sulfuric Acid

Two sulfuric acids → **2H$_2$SO$_4$**

Two hydrogens · One sulfur · Four oxygens

Calcium Nitrate

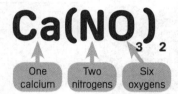

Ca(NO)$_3$$_2$

One calcium · Two nitrogens · Six oxygens

(NO$_3$)$_2$ means 2 × NO$_3$, i.e. NO$_3$ + NO$_3$.

Displayed Formulae

A **displayed formula** shows you the arrangement of atoms in a compound.

A displayed formula shows:

- the different types of atom in the molecule, (e.g. carbon, hydrogen)
- the number of each different type of atom
- the bonds between the atoms.

Ethanol, C$_2$H$_5$OH

$$H-\overset{\overset{\displaystyle H}{|}}{\underset{\underset{\displaystyle H}{|}}{C}}-\overset{\overset{\displaystyle H}{|}}{\underset{\underset{\displaystyle H}{|}}{C}}-O-H$$

Covalent bond

Ethene, C$_2$H$_4$

$$\overset{H}{\underset{H}{}}C=C\overset{H}{\underset{H}{}}$$

Equations

In a chemical reaction the substances that you start with are called **reactants**. During the reaction, the atoms in the reactants are rearranged to form new substances called **products**.

We use equations to show what has happened during a chemical reaction. The reactants are on the left of the equation and the products are on the right.

No atoms are lost or gained during a chemical reaction so the equation must be balanced: there must always be the same number and type of atoms on both sides of the equation.

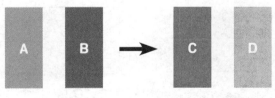

A   B → C   D

Reactants   Products

Fundamental Chemical Concepts

Writing Balanced Equations

Example 1

1. Write a word equation.
2. Substitute in symbols and formulae.
3. Balance the equation.
   - First, you need to add another MgO to the product side to balance the Os.
   - You now need to add another Mg on the reactant side to balance the Mgs.
   - There are two magnesium atoms and two oxygen atoms on each side – it's balanced.
4. Write a balanced symbol equation.

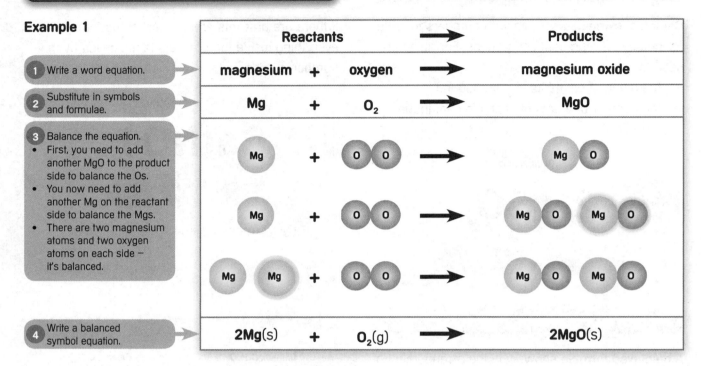

Reactants			→	Products
magnesium	+	oxygen	→	magnesium oxide
Mg	+	O_2	→	MgO
$2Mg(s)$	+	$O_2(g)$	→	$2MgO(s)$

When you write equations, you may be asked to include the **state symbols**: (aq) for aqueous solutions (dissolved in water), (g) for gases, (l) for liquids and (s) for solids.

HT You should be able to balance equations by looking at the formulae (i.e. without drawing the atoms).

1. Write a word equation.
2. Substitute in symbols and formulae.
3. Balance the equation.
4. Write a balanced symbol equation with state symbols.

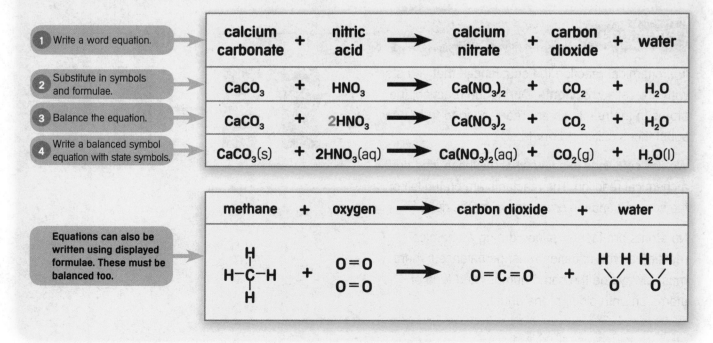

calcium carbonate	+	nitric acid	→	calcium nitrate	+	carbon dioxide	+	water
$CaCO_3$	+	HNO_3	→	$Ca(NO_3)_2$	+	CO_2	+	H_2O
$CaCO_3$	+	$2HNO_3$	→	$Ca(NO_3)_2$	+	CO_2	+	H_2O
$CaCO_3(s)$	+	$2HNO_3(aq)$	→	$Ca(NO_3)_2(aq)$	+	$CO_2(g)$	+	$H_2O(l)$

Equations can also be written using displayed formulae. These must be balanced too.

methane	+	oxygen	→	carbon dioxide	+	water

Fundamental Chemical Concepts

Compounds and their Formulae

Acids

Ethanoic acid	CH_3COOH
Hydrochloric acid	HCl
(HT) Nitric acid	HNO_3
(HT) Sulfuric acid	H_2SO_4

Carbonates

Calcium carbonate	$CaCO_3$
Copper(II) carbonate	$CuCO_3$
(HT) Magnesium carbonate	$MgCO_3$
(HT) Sodium carbonate	Na_2CO_3
(HT) Zinc carbonate	$ZnCO_3$

Chlorides

Ammonium chloride	NH_4Cl
(HT) Calcium chloride	$CaCl_2$
(HT) Magnesium chloride	$MgCl_2$
Potassium chloride	KCl
Silver chloride	$AgCl$
Sodium chloride	$NaCl$

Oxides

Aluminium oxide	Al_2O_3
Copper(II) oxide	CuO
Iron(II) oxide	FeO
(HT) Magnesium oxide	MgO
(HT) Manganese oxide	MnO_2
(HT) Sulfur dioxide	SO_2
(HT) Zinc oxide	ZnO

Hydroxides

Copper(II) hydroxide	$Cu(OH)_2$
Iron(II) hydroxide	$Fe(OH)_2$
(HT) Potassium hydroxide	KOH
(HT) Sodium hydroxide	$NaOH$

Sulfates

(HT) Ammonium sulfate	$(NH_4)_2SO_4$
(HT) Magnesium sulfate	$MgSO_4$
(HT) Potassium sulfate	K_2SO_4
(HT) Sodium sulfate	Na_2SO_4
(HT) Zinc sulfate	$ZnSO_4$

Others

Ammonia	NH_3
Calcium hydrogencarbonate	$Ca(HCO_3)_2$
Carbon dioxide	CO_2
Carbon monoxide	CO
Chlorine	Cl_2
Ethane	C_2H_6
(HT) Ethanol	C_2H_5OH
(HT) Glucose	$C_6H_{12}O_6$
Hydrogen	H_2
Methane	CH_4
Oxygen	O_2
(HT) Silver nitrate	$AgNO_3$
Water	H_2O

Quick Test

1. What are the negative particles in an atom called?
2. Where are the protons and neutrons found in an atom?
3. What is an ion?
4. What three things can displayed formulae tell you?

C1 Making Crude Oil Useful

Fossil Fuels

Crude oil, coal and natural gas are all **fossil fuels**.

Fossil fuels are:

- **formed naturally** over millions of years
- **finite** and **non-renewable** because they are used up much faster than new supplies can be formed – they will be used up in the future
- all easily extracted.

Crude oil can be used as a source of fuel or chemicals. But it is finite, which means it is being used up much faster than it's being replaced. Scientists are now looking for alternatives for crude oil.

Crude Oil

Crude oil is found in the Earth's crust. It can be pumped to the surface.

Crude oil is transported to refineries through pipelines or in oil tankers.

Accidents can cause oil spills from a tanker and the oil floats on the sea's surface as a **slick**. This can harm wildlife and damage beaches.

The oil can affect lots of wildlife, including birds. The birds' feathers get stuck together and the birds may die.

Detergents are used to break up oil slicks, but these chemicals are toxic and can harm or kill wildlife.

Fractional Distillation

Crude oil is a mixture of many **hydrocarbons**. A hydrocarbon is a molecule that contains **only hydrogen** and **carbon** atoms.

Different hydrocarbons have different **boiling points**. This means that crude oil can be separated into useful **fractions** (parts) that contain mixtures of hydrocarbons with similar boiling points. The process used is **fractional distillation**.

The crude oil is heated in a **fractionating column**. The column has a **temperature gradient**, which makes it hotter at the bottom of the column than at the top:

- Fractions with **low boiling points** leave at the **top** of the fractionating column.
- Fractions with **high boiling points** leave at the **bottom** of the fractionating column.

One of the fractions is liquefied petroleum gas (LPG). It contains propane and butane, which are gases at room temperature and are bottled.

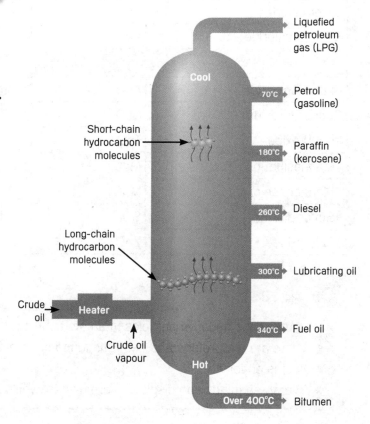

Key Words   Fossil fuel • Non-renewable • Hydrocarbon • Fractional distillation

Cracking

Hydrocarbon molecules can be described as **alkanes** or **alkenes**.

Large alkane molecules can be broken down into smaller, more useful, alkane and alkene molecules.

This industrial process is called **cracking**, and needs a catalyst, a high temperature and a high pressure. In the laboratory, cracking is carried out using the apparatus shown here under atmospheric pressure.

Cracking is used to make more petrol from naphtha. It can also be used to make alkene molecules that may be used to make **polymers**.

There is pressure on these limited resources.

(HT) There isn't enough petrol in crude oil to meet demand. So, cracking is used to change parts of crude oil that can't be used into additional petrol. Crude oil is found in many parts of the world, so oil companies have to work with lots of different countries to extract the oil. Oil is a very valuable resource and is often a source of conflict between nations, and a target for terrorists.

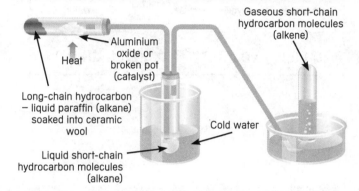

Gaseous short-chain hydrocarbon molecules (alkene)

Aluminium oxide or broken pot (catalyst)

Heat

Long-chain hydrocarbon – liquid paraffin (alkane) soaked into ceramic wool

Cold water

Liquid short-chain hydrocarbon molecules (alkane)

(HT) Forces Between Molecules

In a hydrocarbon molecule there are:
- strong covalent bonds between the atoms in the molecule
- weak **intermolecular** forces (forces of attraction between molecules).

The intermolecular forces between longer hydrocarbons are stronger than the forces between shorter hydrocarbons. When a liquid hydrocarbon is boiled, its molecules move faster and faster until all the intermolecular forces are broken and it becomes a gas.

Small molecules have very weak forces of attraction between them and are easy to overcome by heating. It's the differences in their boiling points which allow us to separate a mixture of hydrocarbons (e.g. crude oil) by the process of **fractional distillation**.

Quick Test

1. What does 'non-renewable' mean?
2. What two elements are contained in hydrocarbons?
3. Which fraction contains propane and butane?
4. Long-chain hydrocarbons often undergo further processing before they can be used.
   a) What is cracking?
   (HT) b) Why is cracking carried out?

C1 Using Carbon Fuels

Combustion

When fuels react with oxygen (in air), they burn and release useful heat energy. This is called **combustion**, and it needs a plentiful supply of oxygen (air).

Many fuels are **hydrocarbons**. **Complete combustion** of a hydrocarbon, e.g. methane, in air produces carbon dioxide and water.

methane	+	oxygen	$\longrightarrow$	carbon dioxide	+	water

(HT) $CH_4(g) + 2O_2(g) \longrightarrow CO_2(g) + 2H_2O(l)$

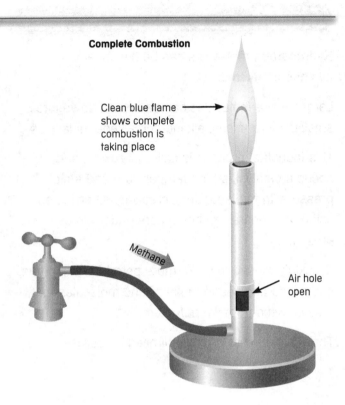

Complete Combustion

Clean blue flame shows complete combustion is taking place

Methane

Air hole open

Incomplete Combustion

When fuels burn without enough oxygen, then **incomplete combustion** happens. Some heat energy is released, but not as much as complete combustion.

Incomplete combustion of a hydrocarbon produces carbon monoxide (a poisonous gas). This is why gas appliances should be serviced regularly.

methane	+	oxygen	$\longrightarrow$	carbon monoxide	+	water

(HT) $2CH_4(g) + 3O_2(g) \longrightarrow 2CO(g) + 4H_2O(l)$

When very little oxygen is present, incomplete combustion of a hydrocarbon produces carbon (soot) and water.

methane	+	oxygen	$\longrightarrow$	carbon	+	water

(HT) $CH_4(g) + O_2(g) \longrightarrow C(s) + 2H_2O(l)$

Incomplete Combustion

The yellow flame makes lots of soot

Yellow flame shows incomplete combustion is taking place

Methane

Air hole closed

Combustion • Complete combustion • Incomplete combustion

Testing the Products of Combustion

This diagram shows that water and carbon dioxide are made when a hydrocarbon combusts in lots of oxygen.

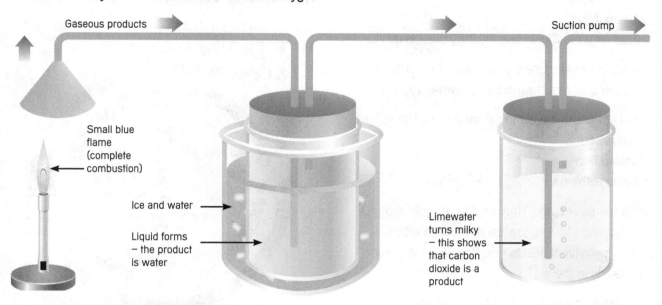

Gaseous products

Suction pump

Small blue flame (complete combustion)

Ice and water

Liquid forms – the product is water

Limewater turns milky – this shows that carbon dioxide is a product

Choosing a Fuel

When choosing a fuel you need to think about:

- **Energy value** – how much energy is released from a gram of fuel?
- **Availability** – how easy is it to get the fuel?
- **Ease of storage** – how easy is it to store the fuel?
- **Cost** – how much fuel do you get for your money?
- **Toxicity** – is the fuel (or its combustion products) poisonous?
- **Pollution** – do the combustion products cause pollution?
- **Ease of use** – is it easy to control and is special equipment needed?

When using a fuel, you want complete combustion to happen because:

- less soot is produced
- more heat energy is released
- no carbon monoxide is made.

(HT) As the world's population increases and more countries like India and China become industrialised, the demand for **fossil fuels** continues to grow.

Quick Test

1. What type of combustion produces carbon monoxide?
2. What colour is a Bunsen burner flame during complete combustion?
3. Which gas in the air is used for combustion?
4. (HT) Write a balanced symbol equation for the complete combustion of methane (CH_4).
5. (HT) Write a balanced symbol equation for the incomplete combustion of methane (CH_4).

C1 Clean Air

The Atmosphere Today

Today, clean dry air contains about:

- 78% **nitrogen**
- 21% **oxygen**
- 1% other gases, including 0.035% carbon dioxide.

The levels of these gases stay about the same. Air also contains different amounts of **water vapour**.

The levels of gas in the **atmosphere** are maintained by:

- **respiration**
- **combustion**
- **photosynthesis**.

All living things **respire**. They take in oxygen and give out carbon dioxide. Respiration and **combustion** decrease the oxygen levels and increase the carbon dioxide levels in the air.

Plants **photosynthesise**: they take in carbon dioxide and release oxygen. Photosynthesis and respiration

balance out, so the levels of carbon dioxide and oxygen in the air stay almost the same.

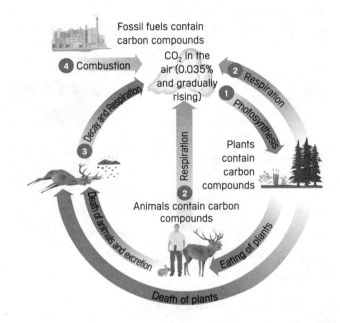

Changing Levels of Gases

The Earth's atmosphere hasn't always been the same as it is today. It has gradually changed over billions of years.

The earliest atmosphere contained ammonia and carbon dioxide. These gases came **from inside the Earth** and were **released** through **volcanoes**.

As plants developed, photosynthesis began and this **reduced** the amount of **carbon dioxide** and **increased** the amount of **oxygen** in the atmosphere.

(HT) The following is one theory used to explain how Earth's atmosphere evolved:

1. A hot volcanic Earth **released gases** from the crust into the atmosphere. So, the initial atmosphere was made up of ammonia, carbon dioxide and water vapour.

2. As the Earth **cooled**, its surface temperature gradually fell below 100°C and the water vapour **condensed** into liquid water. These newly formed oceans removed some carbon dioxide by dissolving the gas.

3. The levels of nitrogen in the atmosphere increased as **nitrifying bacteria** released nitrogen. This gas is quite unreactive.

4. The level of oxygen in the atmosphere started to increase with the development of primitive plants that could photosynthesise. This **removed carbon dioxide** from the atmosphere, and **added oxygen**.

Air Pollution

The air is becoming increasingly **polluted** with harmful gases due to human actions:

- **Sulfur dioxide** is made when fossil fuels that contain sulfur impurities are burned. It causes acid rain which:
  - kills plants and aquatic life
  - erodes stonework and corrodes ironwork.

- **Carbon monoxide** is a poisonous gas formed from incomplete combustion in a car engine.
- **Oxides of nitrogen** are formed in car engines. They cause photochemical smog and acid rain.

(HT) Nitrogen and oxygen from the air react in the hot car engine to make nitrogen monoxide (NO) and nitrogen dioxide (NO_2).

(HT) Human Influence on the Atmosphere

Three key factors have affected the balance of carbon dioxide that is removed from, and returned to, the atmosphere:

1. **Burning of fossil fuels** is increasing the amount of carbon dioxide in the atmosphere.
2. **Deforestation** on large areas of the Earth's surface means the amount of photosynthesis is reduced so less carbon dioxide is removed from the atmosphere.
3. **Increase in world population** has directly and indirectly contributed to the above factors.

Reducing Pollution

It's important to **reduce** air pollution as much as possible because it can **damage** our surroundings and can **affect** people's health.

Carbon monoxide can be changed into **carbon dioxide** by a **catalytic converter**.

(HT) Catalytic converters contain catalysts which help the polluting chemicals in exhaust gases to react with oxygen. Less harmful gases like carbon dioxide are produced instead. This helps to reduce the amount of pollutants released into the atmosphere.

carbon monoxide	+	nitrogen oxide	→	nitrogen	+	carbon dioxide
$2CO$	+	$2NO$	→	N_2	+	$2CO_2$

Quick Test

1. What are the two main gases found in dry air?
2. Which two processes decrease oxygen levels in the atmosphere?
3. Which two gases were contained in the Earth's early atmosphere?
4. What types of pollution are caused by oxides of nitrogen?

C1 Making Polymers

Hydrocarbons

Hydrocarbons are compounds that contain only carbon and hydrogen:

- Carbon atoms can make four bonds each.
- Hydrogen atoms can make one bond each.

(HT) To make a hydrocarbon, hydrogen atoms react with carbon atoms to form **covalent** bonds. When this happens, carbon atoms share a pair of electrons with hydrogen atoms to make a covalent bond.

Methane, CH_4

$$H - \underset{\underset{H}{|}}{\overset{\overset{H}{|}}{C}} - H$$

Alkanes

When a hydrocarbon chain has only **single covalent bonds**, it is called an **alkane**. All of the carbon atoms make four single covalent bonds. The main chain will contain only single carbon–carbon (C–C) bonds. The name of an alkane always ends in **-ane**.

(HT) Alkanes contain only single covalent bonds – they are described as saturated hydrocarbons. (They have the maximum number of hydrogen atoms per carbon atom in the molecule.)

This table shows the displayed and molecular formulae for the first four members of the alkane series.

Alkane	Methane, CH_4	Ethane, C_2H_6	Propane, C_3H_8	Butane, C_4H_{10}
Displayed Formula	$H-\underset{\underset{H}{\vert}}{\overset{\overset{H}{\vert}}{C}}-H$	$H-\underset{\underset{H}{\vert}}{\overset{\overset{H}{\vert}}{C}}-\underset{\underset{H}{\vert}}{\overset{\overset{H}{\vert}}{C}}-H$	$H-\underset{\underset{H}{\vert}}{\overset{\overset{H}{\vert}}{C}}-\underset{\underset{H}{\vert}}{\overset{\overset{H}{\vert}}{C}}-\underset{\underset{H}{\vert}}{\overset{\overset{H}{\vert}}{C}}-H$	$H-\underset{\underset{H}{\vert}}{\overset{\overset{H}{\vert}}{C}}-\underset{\underset{H}{\vert}}{\overset{\overset{H}{\vert}}{C}}-\underset{\underset{H}{\vert}}{\overset{\overset{H}{\vert}}{C}}-\underset{\underset{H}{\vert}}{\overset{\overset{H}{\vert}}{C}}-H$

Alkenes

When a hydrocarbon chain has **one or more double carbon–carbon (C=C) covalent bonds**, it's called an **alkene**. Double bonds have two shared pairs of electrons. The name of an alkene always ends in **-ene**.

(HT) Alkenes have at least one double covalent bond, so the carbon atom isn't bonded to the maximum number of hydrogen atoms. Alkenes are described as being unsaturated.

This table shows the displayed and molecular formulae for the first three members of the alkene series.

Alkene	Ethene, C_2H_4	Propene, C_3H_6	Butene, C_4H_8
Displayed Formula	$\overset{H}{\underset{H}{}}C=C\overset{H}{\underset{H}{}}$	$\overset{H}{\underset{H}{}}C=C-\underset{\underset{H}{\vert}}{\overset{\overset{H}{\vert}}{C}}-H$	$\overset{H}{\underset{H}{}}C=C-\underset{\underset{H}{\vert}}{\overset{\overset{H}{\vert}}{C}}-\underset{\underset{H}{\vert}}{\overset{\overset{H}{\vert}}{C}}-H$

Key Words **Covalent • Saturated • Unsaturated**

Test for Alkenes

A simple test to distinguish between alkenes and alkanes is to add bromine water:

- Alkenes decolourise bromine water. (The unsaturated alkene reacts with it.)
- Alkanes have no effect on bromine water, i.e. the bromine water stays orange. (The saturated alkane can't react with it.)

(HT) This reaction is a test for unsaturation. It is an addition reaction between bromine water and the C=C to make a colourless dibromo compound.

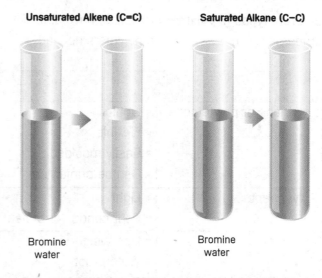

Unsaturated Alkene (C=C)   Saturated Alkane (C–C)

Bromine water   Bromine water

Polymerisation

The alkenes made by cracking are small molecules which can be used as **monomers**. The double bonds in alkenes are easily broken, so monomers can be joined together to make **polymers** (large, long-chain molecules). Molecules in plastic are called polymers.

When the alkenes join together making a polymer, the reaction is called **polymerisation**. This process needs **high pressure** and a **catalyst**. You could use displayed formulae to show a polymerisation reaction, for example, ethene monomers making poly(ethene):

Ethene monomers (unsaturated)   Poly(ethene) polymers (saturated)

… and many more …   … and on and on …

But, it's better to use the standard way of displaying a polymer formula:

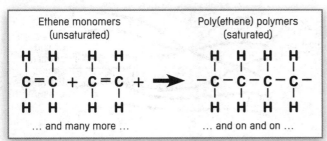

(HT) Polymerisation involves the reaction of many unsaturated monomer molecules, i.e. alkenes, to form a saturated polymer. You should be able to construct the displayed formula of:

- a **polymer** if you're given the displayed formula of a monomer, e.g. propene monomer to poly(propene) polymer

Monomer   Polymer

- a **monomer** if you're given the displayed formula of a polymer, e.g. poly(propene) polymer to propene monomer.

Polymer   Monomer

C1 Designer Polymers

Polymers

Different types of **polymers** (plastics) have different properties. The uses of these polymers depend on their properties. This table lists some polymers' properties and uses.

Polymer	Properties	Uses
Polythene or poly(ethene)	• Light • Flexible • Easily moulded • Can be printed on	• Plastic bags – the plastic is flexible and light. • Moulded containers – the plastic is easily moulded.
Polystyrene	• Light • Poor conductor of heat	• Insulation – the plastic is a poor conductor of heat.
Polyester	• Lightweight • Waterproof • Tough • Can be coloured	• Clothing – the plastic can be made into fibres, is lightweight, tough, waterproof and can be coloured. • Bottles – the plastic is lightweight and waterproof.

HT Structure of Plastics

Polymers like PVC are made of tangled very long chain molecules. The atoms are held together by strong **covalent** bonds.

Plastics that have weak forces between polymer molecules (**intermolecular forces**):
- have low melting points
- can be stretched easily because the polymer molecules can slide over each other.

Plastics that have strong forces between the polymer molecules (covalent bonds or cross-linking bridges):
- have high melting points
- are rigid and can't be stretched.

Plastic with Weak Intermolecular Forces

Long chain of molecules

Weak intermolecular force between chains

Plastic with Strong Intermolecular Forces (Cross-links)

Long chain of molecules

Strong covalent bond between chains

Nylon

Nylon:
- is lightweight
- is tough
- is waterproof
- blocks UV light (harmful sunlight).

Nylon's properties make it ideal for outdoor clothing.

But, although it's waterproof (i.e. keeps you dry) it doesn't let water vapour escape, so it can be uncomfortable if you become hot and start to sweat (perspire).

Gore-Tex®

Gore-Tex® is a breathable material made from nylon. It has all of the advantages of nylon, but it's also treated with a material that allows sweat (water vapour) to escape whilst preventing rain from getting in. This is more comfortable than nylon, as it stops you from getting wet when you sweat.

(HT) In Gore-Tex®, the nylon fibres are coated (laminated) with a membrane of poly(tetrafluoroethene) (PTFE) or polyurethane. This makes the holes in the fabric much smaller.

The coating is used with nylon because it's too weak to be used on its own.

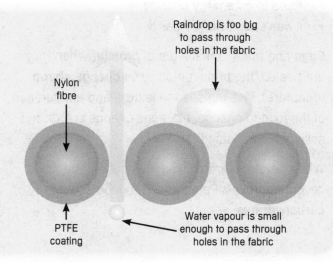

Raindrop is too big to pass through holes in the fabric

Nylon fibre

PTFE coating

Water vapour is small enough to pass through holes in the fabric

Disposing of Polymers

We produce a large amount of plastic waste (polymers) which can be difficult to dispose of and causes litter in the streets.

There are three choices for disposal of plastic waste, but they all have disadvantages. See below.

Research is being carried out on the development of **biodegradable** plastics. These plastics contain special parts which dissolve easily and break up the polymer chain. Biodegradable plastics are already being used in dishwasher detergent tablets.

Using **landfill** sites:	**Burning** polymers:	**Recycling** polymers:
• Most plastics are non-biodegradable, i.e. they will not be broken down by bacteria or decay. • Wastes valuable resources. • Landfill sites get filled up very quickly, i.e. they waste land.	• Produces air pollution. • Some plastics produce toxic fumes when they are burned, for example, burning poly(chloroethene) (PVC) produces hydrogen chloride gas. • Wastes valuable resources.	• Different types of plastic need to be recycled separately – sorting plastics into groups can be time-consuming and expensive.

Quick Test

1. What is a polymer?
2. Name the polymer made from ethene.
3. Give two reasons why polyester is used in clothing.

C1 Cooking and Food Additives

Cooking Food

Cooking food causes a chemical change to take place. When a chemical change happens:

- **new substances** are formed
- there is an **energy change**
- it **can't be reversed** easily.

Eggs and **meat** contain lots of **protein**. When they are heated, the protein molecules **change shape** (**denature**). This causes the texture and appearance of the food to change, e.g. eggs change colour and solidify when heated.

When **potatoes** are cooked they soften and the flavour improves. Potatoes are a good source of **carbohydrates**.

(HT) Potatoes and other vegetables are plants, so their cells have a rigid cell wall.

During cooking, the heat breaks down the cell wall and the cells become soft. Starch grains swell up and are released, so your body can easily digest them.

Eggs and meat contain protein. Denaturing causes the protein molecules to change shape during cooking; it is an irreversible process.

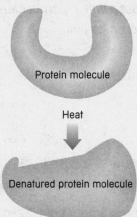

Protein molecule

Heat

Denatured protein molecule

Baking Powder

Baking powder contains **sodium hydrogen carbonate**. When it is heated, it **decomposes** (breaks down) to make sodium carbonate and water, and **carbon dioxide** gas is given off:

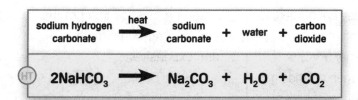

| sodium hydrogen carbonate | $\xrightarrow{heat}$ | sodium carbonate | + | water | + | carbon dioxide |

(HT) $2NaHCO_3 \longrightarrow Na_2CO_3 + H_2O + CO_2$

Baking powder is added to cake mixture because as the mixture is heated, the carbon dioxide gas that is released causes the cake to **rise**.

Limewater (calcium hydroxide solution) can be used to test for carbon dioxide. If carbon dioxide is present, the limewater will change from colourless to **milky**.

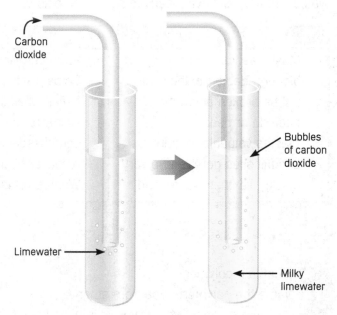

Carbon dioxide

Limewater

Bubbles of carbon dioxide

Milky limewater

Key Words   **Decomposition**

Additives

Food **additives** are substances that are put into food to improve it.

A small number of people are **allergic** to certain food additives, i.e. they are harmed by them.

There are different types of food additives:

- **Antioxidants** stop food reacting with oxygen in the air and increase the shelf life.
- **Food colours** improve the appearance of food.
- **Flavour enhancers** bring out the flavour of a food without adding a taste of their own.
- **Emulsifiers** help mix oil and water, which would normally separate, e.g. in mayonnaise.

NUTRITION INFORMATION

Typical Values	Per 100g
Energy	182kJ
Protein	0.8g
Carbohydrates	6.0g
Fat	1.8g
Fibre	0.6g
Sodium	0.3g

Suitable for vegetarians
Suitable for coeliacs

Emulsifiers

Oil and water don't mix, so **emulsifiers** are used. The molecules in an emulsifier have two ends: one end likes to be in water (**hydrophilic**) and the other end likes to be in oil (**hydrophobic**). The emulsifier joins the droplets together and keeps them mixed.

(HT) The **hydrophilic** end of an emulsifier molecule attracts to the water molecules. The **hydrophobic** end of the emulsifier molecule attracts to the oil molecules. This attraction holds the oil and water molecules together, stopping them from separating.

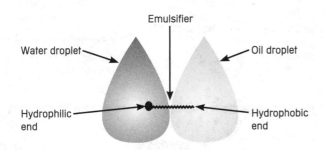

Water droplet · Emulsifier · Oil droplet · Hydrophilic end · Hydrophobic end

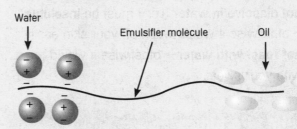

Water · Emulsifier molecule · Oil

Quick Test

1. Give an example of a food that is high in protein.
2. Baking powder is put into cakes to make them rise.
   a) What is the name of the chemical in baking powder?
   b) What chemical change happens when baking powder is heated?
   c) Write a word equation for the reaction when baking powder is heated in a cake.
   d) Which product of this reaction causes cakes to rise?
3. What is meant by 'denaturing'?

C1 Smells

Perfumes

Some cosmetics come from **natural sources**, such as plants and animals. Examples of perfumes from natural sources include lavender, musk and rose.

Cosmetics can also be manufactured. Manufactured perfumes are known as **synthetic perfumes**.

Esters are a family of **compounds** often used as perfumes. An ester is made by reacting an alcohol with an organic acid to produce an ester and water.

Esters can also be used as solvents.

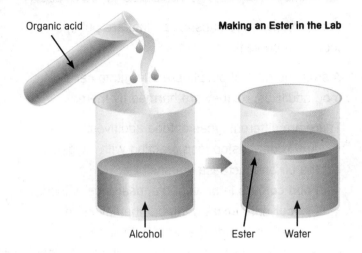

Organic acid

Making an Ester in the Lab

Alcohol   Ester   Water

Properties of Perfume

Smells are made of molecules which travel up your nose and stimulate sense cells.

A perfume must smell nice, and must:
- **evaporate easily** – so it can travel to your nose
- **not be toxic** – so it doesn't poison you
- **not irritate** – otherwise it would be uncomfortable on your skin
- **not dissolve in water** (i.e. it must be **insoluble**) – otherwise it would wash off your skin easily
- **not react with water** – otherwise it would react with your sweat.

(HT) Perfumes are **volatile**, which means they evaporate easily.

The molecules of perfume are held together by weak forces of attraction. The molecules that have lots of energy can easily overcome the weak forces of attraction and escape.

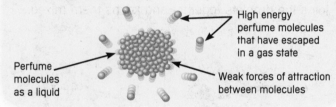

High energy perfume molecules that have escaped in a gas state

Perfume molecules as a liquid

Weak forces of attraction between molecules

Testing Perfumes

Perfumes and cosmetics need to be tested to make sure they are safe to use. This testing is sometimes done on animals, although testing on animals has been banned in the EU.

(HT) **Advantage** of animal testing:
- It can prevent humans from being harmed.

Disadvantages of animal testing:
- It's cruel to animals.
- Animals don't have the same body chemistry as humans, so test results might not be useful.

Describing Solutions

Here are some words used to describe substances:

- **Soluble substances** are substances that dissolve in a liquid, e.g. nail varnish is soluble in ethyl ethanoate (nail varnish remover).
- **Insoluble substances** are substances that don't dissolve in a liquid, e.g. nail varnish is insoluble in water.
- A **solvent** is the liquid into which a substance is dissolved, e.g. ethyl ethanoate is a solvent. (An ester can be used as a solvent.)
- The **solute** is the substance that gets dissolved, e.g. the nail varnish is a solute.
- A **solution** is what you get when you mix a solvent and a solute; it will not separate out.

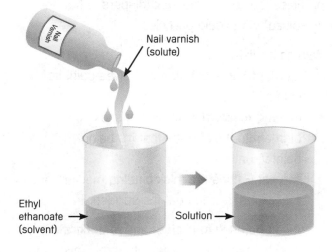

Nail varnish (solute)

Ethyl ethanoate (solvent)

Solution

Solvents

Nail varnish dissolves in nail varnish remover (ethyl ethanoate), but not in water.

(HT) Nail varnish will not dissolve in water because:

- the attraction between water molecules is stronger than the attraction between water molecules and nail varnish molecules
- the attraction between the molecules in nail varnish is stronger than the attraction between water molecules and nail varnish molecules.

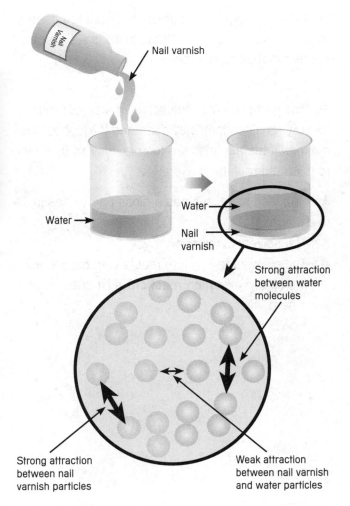

Nail varnish

Water

Water

Nail varnish

Strong attraction between water molecules

Strong attraction between nail varnish particles

Weak attraction between nail varnish and water particles

C1 Paints and Pigments

Paint

Paint is a colloid. Colloids are made of small, solid particles that are mixed well (dispersed but not dissolved) with liquid particles.

Paint is a mixture of:

- **pigment** – a substance that gives paint its colour
- **binding medium** – an oil that sticks the pigment to the surface that it's being painted onto
- **solvent** – thins the thick binding medium and makes it easier to coat the surface.

Paint can be used to **protect** and to **decorate** a surface. It coats the surface with a thin layer and dries when the **solvent evaporates**.

The solvent in **emulsion** paint is water.

In oil-based paints, the pigment is dispersed in an oil (the binding medium). Often, there is a solvent present that dissolves the oil.

HT The particle size of the solids in a colloid must be very small so they stay scattered throughout the mixture. If the particles are too big, they settle down to the bottom of the mixture.

An oil-based paint, such as a gloss paint, dries in two stages:

1. The solvent **evaporates** away.
2. The oil-binding medium reacts with oxygen in the air (an **oxidation reaction**) as it dries to form a hard layer.

Pigment • Emulsion

Special Pigments

Thermochromic **pigments** change colour when they are heated or cooled.

These pigments can be used:
- to coat kettles and cups to indicate the temperature
- in mood rings
- in toys and cutlery for babies to warn if food or bath water is too hot.

Phosphorescent pigments glow in the dark. They absorb and store energy and then release it as light when it's dark.

(HT) A thermochromic pigment can be added to acrylic paints, which makes the paint change through more colours.

The first 'glow in the dark' paints were made using radioactive materials as pigments and were used for things like watches. But, they were dangerous as they exposed people to too much radiation.

Phosphorescent pigments aren't radioactive, so they are much safer to use.

Quick Test

1. Give an example of a cosmetic from a natural source.
2. Why is it important that perfumes do not dissolve in water?
3. What is a colloid?
4. What are the three main parts that make up a paint?
5. What is paint used for?
6. (HT) How does oil-based paint dry?

Key Words   **Thermochromic • Phosphorescent**

1 **a)** Crude oil is a mixture of hydrocarbons.

Explain how fractional distillation separates the fractions in crude oil. **[2]**

b) What is cracking and why is it used? **[2]**

c) Explain why small hydrocarbon molecules have a lower boiling point than large hydrocarbon molecules. **[2]**

2 Clean air contains a mixture of gases. The proportions of these gases are shown in the pie chart below.

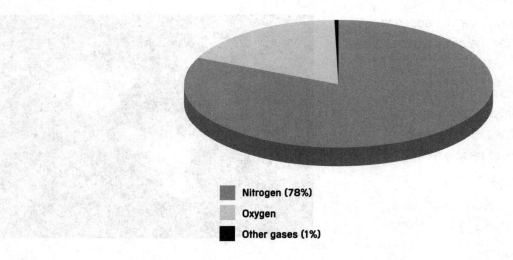

- ■ Nitrogen (78%)
- ■ Oxygen
- ■ Other gases (1%)

a) Which gas makes up most of the air? **[1]**

b) What percentage of the air is made up of oxygen? **[1]**

c) Give an example of a gas that would be found in 'other gases'. **[1]**

3 The Bunsen burner has two flames: the yellow safety flame and the blue heating flame.

a) Explain why a blue Bunsen flame is hotter than a yellow Bunsen flame. [1]

b) Write the word equation for the complete combustion of methane. [1]

4 Alkenes can be used to make polymers (plastics).

a) What is a monomer? [1]

b) Describe the conditions needed for the polymerisation of an alkene. [2]

(HT)

5 Gore-Tex® is a breathable fabric, used to make outdoor clothes. Explain how a Gore-Tex® coat is waterproof but allows water vapour to escape from inside. [3]

6 Emulsifiers are molecules that keep oil and water mixed. Explain how an emulsifier molecule keeps oil and water mixed. [6]

✎ *The quality of your written communication will be assessed in your answer to this question.*

C2 The Structure of the Earth

Structure of the Earth

The **Earth** is made of a layered structure. It has a:

- thin, rocky **crust**
- **mantle**
- **core** (containing iron).

It's difficult to collect information about the structure of the Earth. The deepest mines and holes drilled into the crust are only a few kilometres into the thick crust.

Scientists have to rely on studying the **seismic waves** (vibrations) caused by **earthquakes** to understand the structure of the Earth.

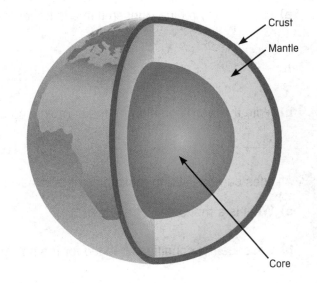

Crust

Mantle

Core

Movement of the Lithosphere

The Earth's **lithosphere** is the relatively cold, rigid outer part of the Earth, made of the crust and top part of the mantle.

The top of the lithosphere is 'cracked' into several large interlocking pieces called **tectonic plates**:

- **Oceanic plates** sit under the ocean.
- **Continental plates** form the continents.

The plates sit on top of the mantle because they are **less dense** than the mantle. Plates move very slowly (about 2.5cm per year). These movements cause **earthquakes** and **volcanoes** at the **boundaries** between plates.

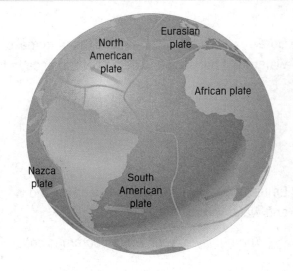

North American plate

Eurasian plate

African plate

Nazca plate

South American plate

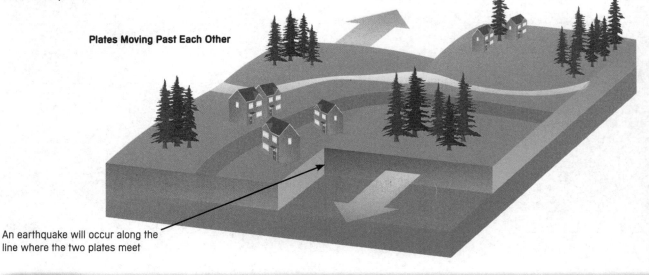

Plates Moving Past Each Other

An earthquake will occur along the line where the two plates meet

Key Words   Crust • Mantle • Core • Seismic wave • Lithosphere • Tectonic plate

Just below the crust, the **mantle** is relatively cold and rigid. At greater depths, the mantle becomes hot and fluid, which means that it can flow. There are **convection currents**, formed by **heat** released from radioactive decay in the core.

Convection currents cause **magma** (molten rock) to **rise** to the surface at the boundaries of plates.

When the molten rock solidifies, new **igneous rock** is formed. This slow movement of the magma causes the plates to **move**.

Oceanic crust has a higher **density** than continental crust. When an oceanic plate collides with a continental plate, it dips down and **slides under** it. This is called subduction. The oceanic plate is **partially re-melted** as it goes under the continental plate.

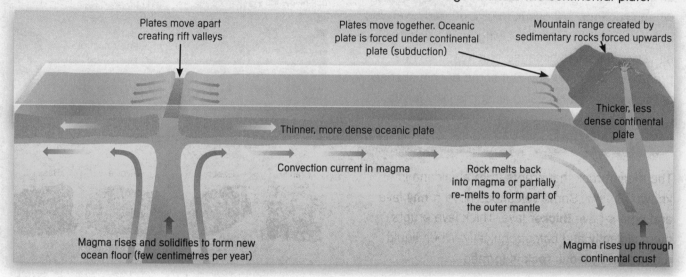

Plates move apart creating rift valleys

Plates move together. Oceanic plate is forced under continental plate (subduction)

Mountain range created by sedimentary rocks forced upwards

Thinner, more dense oceanic plate

Thicker, less dense continental plate

Convection current in magma

Rock melts back into magma or partially re-melts to form part of the outer mantle

Magma rises and solidifies to form new ocean floor (few centimetres per year)

Magma rises up through continental crust

Developing a Theory

Many theories (ideas) have been put forward to explain changes in the Earth's surface. Earth scientists now accept the theory of **plate tectonics**.

HT In 1914, a scientist called Alfred Wegener suggested that the surface of the Earth was changing. He developed the idea that, millions of years ago, all the continents were joined together. Wegener noticed several features on the surface of the Earth:

- The continents look like they would fit together like a **jigsaw**.
- The geology of Scotland and Canada was similar, as was the geology of Africa and South America.
- **Similar animal species** were found on either side of the Atlantic, e.g. caribou in Canada and reindeer in Scandinavia.

This theory is widely accepted as it explains a range of evidence and has been discussed and tested by many scientists.

Initially, Wegener's ideas were not accepted by other scientists. But Wegener's theory was supported by studies in the 1960s which looked at new rock formed at oceanic plate boundaries. The studies showed that:

- the plates are moving apart
- the age of rock increases as you move away from the boundary.

So Wegener's theory of plate tectonics has gradually become accepted.

C2 The Structure of the Earth

Volcanoes

Volcanoes form at places where **magma** (molten rock underneath the Earth's surface) can find its way through weaknesses in the Earth's crust. This is often at plate boundaries or where the crust is very thin. The magma rises through the crust because it has a **lower density** than the crust.

Geologists study volcanoes to help understand the **structure** of the **Earth**. They also aim to **predict** when **eruptions** will occur, to give an early warning to people who live nearby. Living near a volcano can be very dangerous because eruptions can't be predicted with accuracy. But some people choose to live there because volcanic soil is very **fertile**.

(HT) Geologists are now better able to predict eruptions, but they still can't be 100% accurate.

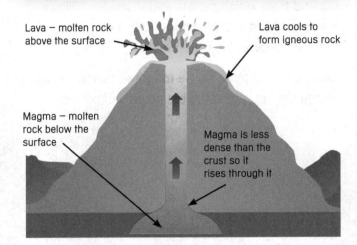

Lava – molten rock above the surface

Lava cools to form igneous rock

Magma – molten rock below the surface

Magma is less dense than the crust so it rises through it

Forming Rock

The molten rock that erupts from a volcano is known as **lava**. Some volcanoes have **runny** lava, and others have **thicker** lava. Thick lava erupts more violently and catastrophically. When liquid rock cools, **igneous rock** is formed.

Igneous rocks are very hard and have interlocking crystals of different sizes:

- **Large crystals** are made when the rock **cools slowly**, as in silica-rich granite and iron-rich gabbro.
- **Small crystals** are made when the rock **cools quickly**, as in silica-rich rhyolite and iron-rich basalt.

Granite   Gabbro   Rhyolite   Basalt

(HT) Volcanoes can produce two types of lava, which affects the type of eruption:

- **Iron-rich basalt** lava is quite runny and has fairly 'safe' eruptions.
- **Silica-rich rhyolite** is thicker. Thicker lava results in more violent and catastrophic eruptions. Rhyolite lava makes pumice, volcanic ash and bombs.

Quick Test

1. What is the lithosphere made from?
2. Why do tectonic plates float on the mantle?
3. Which two natural disasters happen at plate boundaries?
4. What is igneous rock?
5. Explain how rate of cooling affects crystal size in a piece of igneous rock.
6. (HT) What are the properties of iron-rich basalt lava?

Materials from Rocks

Many **construction** materials come from rocks found in the Earth's crust:

- Iron and aluminium are extracted from rocks called **ores**.
- Brick is made by baking clay that has been extracted from the Earth.
- Glass, **concrete** and **cement** are all made from sand (small grains of rock).
- Limestone, marble, granite and **aggregates** (gravel) are types of rock extracted from the Earth. These rocks just need to be shaped to be used as building materials.

Limestone is the easiest to shape because it's the softest. Granite is the hardest to shape.

(HT) Rocks differ in **hardness** because of the ways in which they were made:

- Limestone is a **sedimentary** rock.
- Marble is a **metamorphic** rock made from limestone that has been put under pressure and heated, which makes it harder.
- Granite is an **igneous** rock.

Limestone, Cement and Concrete

Limestone and marble are mainly made of **calcium carbonate** ($CaCO_3$). When calcium carbonate is heated it breaks down into calcium oxide and carbon dioxide:

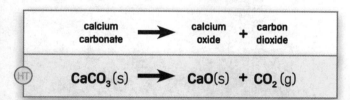

calcium carbonate → calcium oxide + carbon dioxide

(HT) $CaCO_3(s) \longrightarrow CaO(s) + CO_2(g)$

This type of reaction is called a **thermal decomposition** reaction; one material breaks down into two or more new substances when heated.

Clay and limestone can be heated together to make cement. Cement can be mixed with sand, gravel (aggregates) and water and allowed to set to make concrete, which is very hard but not very strong. It can be strengthened by allowing it to set around steel rods to reinforce it. **Reinforced concrete** is a **composite** material.

(HT) A composite material combines the best properties of each component material. Reinforced concrete combines the **strength** and **flexibility** of the steel bars with the **hardness** of the concrete. Reinforced concrete has many **more uses** than ordinary concrete.

Impact on the Environment

Rock is dug out of the ground in mines and quarries. Mining and quarrying companies have to try to **reduce** their **impact** on the local area and **environment** because mines and quarries can:

- be noisy and dusty
- take up land
- change the shape of the landscape
- increase the local road traffic.

A responsible company will also reconstruct, cover up and restore any area that it has worked on.

C2 Metals and Alloys

Copper

Copper is **extracted** from naturally occurring copper **ore** by **heating** it with carbon:

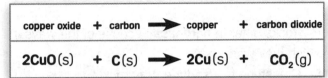

copper oxide	+	carbon	→	copper	+	carbon dioxide
2CuO(s)	+	**C**(s)	→	**2Cu**(s)	+	**CO₂**(g)

The process uses lots of energy, which makes it **expensive**. Oxygen is removed from the copper oxide. This process is called **reduction**. It is **cheaper** to **recycle** copper than to extract it from its ore. Recycling also **conserves** the world's limited supply of copper ore and uses less energy.

But recycling copper can be more difficult if it has other metals stuck to it or mixed with it.

If the copper is very **impure**, it can be purified using **electrolysis** (which is an expensive process) before it can be used again.

Electrolysis

Electrolysis uses an **electric current** to break down compounds into simpler substances.

In **electrolysis**, electricity is passed through a liquid or a solution called an **electrolyte**, e.g. copper(II) sulfate solution, to make simpler substances.

(HT) Electrodes are used to allow the electricity to flow through the electrolyte:

- The **anode** (positive electrode) is made of impure copper.

$$Cu \ - \ 2e^- \ \longrightarrow \ Cu^{2+}$$
This is an oxidation process as electrons are lost.

- The **cathode** (negative electrode) is made of pure copper.

$$Cu^{2+} \ + \ 2e^- \ \longrightarrow \ Cu$$
This is a reduction process as electrons are gained.

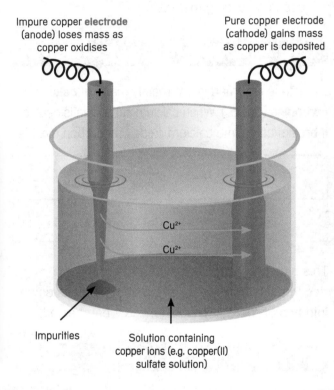

Impure copper **electrode** (anode) loses mass as copper oxidises

Pure copper electrode (cathode) gains mass as copper is deposited

Cu^{2+}

Cu^{2+}

Impurities

Solution containing copper ions (e.g. copper(II) sulfate solution)

Alloys

An **alloy** is a **mixture** of a metal with another element (usually another metal). Bronze and steel are alloys. Alloys improve the **properties** of a metal and make them **more useful** – they are often harder and stronger than the pure metal. For example:

- **amalgam** (made using mercury) is used for fillings in teeth
- **solder** (made of lead and tin) is used to join wires

- **brass** (made of copper and zinc) is used in door handles, coins and musical instruments.

(HT) A **smart alloy** such as nitinol (an alloy of nickel and titanium) can be bent and twisted. Nitinol will return to its original shape when it is heated; it has **shape memory**. This smart alloy is used for the frames of reading glasses.

Materials in a Car

Many different **materials** are used to make cars:
- Nylon **fibre** is used to make the seatbelts because it's strong and flexible.
- **Glass** is used to make the windscreen because it's transparent.
- **Copper** is used for the wiring in the engine because it's a good electrical conductor.
- **Plastic** is used for the trim because it's rigid and doesn't **corrode**.
- **Steel** is used to make the body because it's strong and malleable.
- **Aluminium** is used to make the alloy wheels because it's lightweight and doesn't corrode in moist conditions.

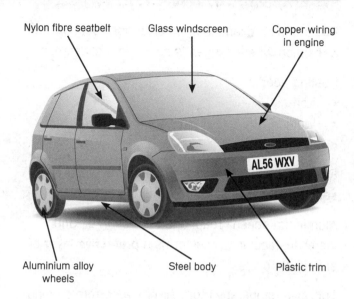

Nylon fibre seatbelt   Glass windscreen   Copper wiring in engine

AL56 WXV

Aluminium alloy wheels   Steel body   Plastic trim

Properties of Metals and Alloys

The table below compares the properties of aluminium and iron:

Property	Aluminium	Iron
Dense	✗	✔
Magnetic	✗	✔
Resists corrosion	✔	✗
Malleable	✔	✔
Conducts electricity	✔	✔

Aluminium can be mixed with other metals, such as copper and magnesium, to make an **alloy**.

Alloys have different **properties** from the metals that they are made from. These properties make the alloy more **useful**.

For example, **steel** is an alloy of iron and carbon. It is used to make cars because it:
- is harder and stronger than iron
- doesn't corrode as fast as iron.

Aluminium is also used to make car bodies. In comparison to steel, it:
- is lighter
- corrodes less
- is more expensive.

(HT) If aluminium is used to make a car, it will have a longer lifetime because aluminium doesn't corrode.

As aluminium is less dense than steel, the car will be lighter so it will have better fuel economy.

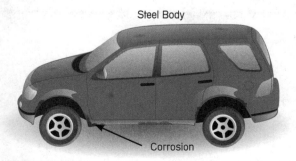

Steel Body

Corrosion

Aluminium Body

C2 Making Cars

Rusting Conditions

Rusting is an example of an **oxidation reaction**, i.e. a reaction where oxygen is added to a substance.

Rusting needs:
- iron
- water
- oxygen (air).

Rusting happens even **faster** when the water is **salty** or is **acid rain**.

Aluminium doesn't react and corrode in air and water. Instead, it quickly forms a **protective layer** of aluminium oxide.

This layer stops any more air or water from coming into contact with the metal. This built-in protection will not flake off.

Oxygen is added to the iron in the presence of water:

iron + oxygen + water ⟶ hydrated iron(III) oxide

Recycling

Most materials used in a car can be **recycled**. Since 2006, the law states that 85% of a car must be able to be recycled; this will increase to 95% in 2015.

Separating all the different materials for recycling can be tricky and time-consuming. But it saves natural resources and avoids disposal problems.

Recycling materials means:
- less quarrying is required
- less energy is used to extract them from ores
- the limited ore reserves will last longer (saves natural resources)
- disposal problems are reduced.

Recycling the plastics and fibres reduces the amount of crude oil needed to make them, and conserves oil reserves.

There are a number of materials in a car that would cause pollution if put into landfill, e.g. lead in the car battery, so recycling also **protects** the **environment**.

Quick Test

1. How are aluminium and iron extracted from the Earth?
2. Give an example of a material that just needs to be shaped before it can be used as a building material.
3. Briefly explain how cement is made.
4. Why is it important to recycle metals?
5. What is an alloy?
6. Why is glass used to make car windscreens?
7. What two elements are needed for iron to rust?

Ammonia

Ammonia (NH_3) is an alkaline gas made from nitrogen and hydrogen. It can be used to make:
- nitric acid
- **fertilisers** (cheap fertilisers are very important in helping to produce enough food for the growing world population).

The reaction which makes ammonia is a **reversible reaction**. So, nitrogen and hydrogen can form ammonia, and ammonia can decompose to make hydrogen and nitrogen.

Reversible reactions have the symbol ⇌ in their equation to show that the reaction can take place in either direction.

The Haber Process

Ammonia is made on a large scale in the **Haber process**. The reactants are:
- nitrogen (from the air)
- hydrogen (from natural gas or the cracking of crude oil).

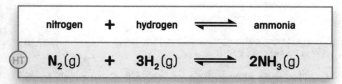

nitrogen + hydrogen ⇌ ammonia

(HT) $N_2(g)$ + $3H_2(g)$ ⇌ $2NH_3(g)$

Optimum conditions aren't used as they would be very expensive to maintain, so a compromise is reached:
- The nitrogen and hydrogen mixture is under a **high pressure** of 200 atmospheres.
- The gases are passed over an iron **catalyst** at **450°C**.

Only about 15% of the reactant gases make ammonia. The unreacted gases are recycled. Ammonia is cooled, condensed and then pumped off as a liquid.

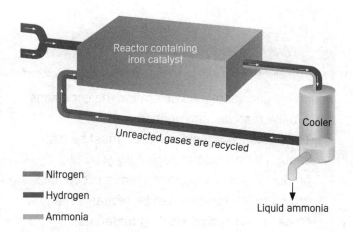

Reactor containing iron catalyst

Cooler

Unreacted gases are recycled

Liquid ammonia

▬ Nitrogen
▬ Hydrogen
▬ Ammonia

Cost and Factors Affecting Cost

The cost of making a new substance depends on:
- the price of energy (gas and electricity)
- labour costs (wages for employees)
- how quickly the new substance can be made (cost of catalyst)
- the cost of starting materials (reactants)
- the cost of equipment needed (plant and machinery).

Factors that affect the cost of making a new substance include:
- the **pressure** – the higher the pressure, the higher the plant cost

- the **temperature** – the higher the temperature, the higher the energy cost
- the **catalysts** – catalysts can be expensive to buy, but production costs are reduced because they increase the rate of reaction
- the **number of people** needed to operate machinery – automation reduces the wages bill
- the **amount of unreacted material** that can be recycled – recycling reduces costs.

Interpreting Data

You need to be able to interpret data percentage **yield** in reversible reactions.

Example

The graph and table show how temperature and pressure affect the rate of reaction in the Haber process.

The information given allows you to work out that the yield falls when temperature is increased, and that the yield increases as pressure increases.

HT You may also be asked to interpret data on other industrial processes in terms of rate, percentage yield and cost.

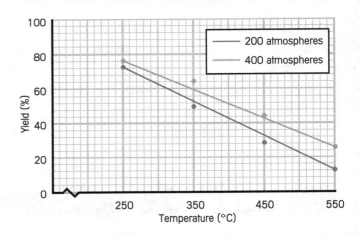

Pressure (Atmospheres)	Yield (%)	Temperature (°C)		
		250	350	450	550
200		73	50	28	13
400		77	65	45	26

HT Economic Considerations

Economic considerations determine the conditions used in the manufacture of chemicals:

- The **percentage yield** achieved must be high enough to produce enough daily yield of product (a low percentage yield is acceptable providing the reaction can be repeated many times with **recycled starting materials**).

- The **rate of reaction** must be high enough to produce enough daily **yield** of product.
- The **optimum conditions** should be used to give the most economical reaction (this could mean a slower reaction or a lower percentage yield at a lower cost).

Economics of the Haber Process

It's important that the **maximum amount** of ammonia is made in the **shortest possible time** at a **reasonable cost**. This requires a **compromise**.

For the Haber process:

- a low temperature increases yield but the reaction is too slow
- a high pressure increases yield but becomes more expensive as yield increases
- a catalyst increases the rate of reaction but doesn't change the percentage yield.

So, a compromise is reached of:
- temperature of 450°C
- pressure of 200 atmospheres
- catalyst of iron.

This gives a fast reaction with an acceptable percentage yield.

Acids, Bases and Indicators

Indicators are chemicals that change colour to show changes in pH. Some indicators, e.g. litmus, have only two colours; others, e.g. **universal indicator**, have a range of colours over different pH values. **Acids** are substances with a pH of **less than 7**. **Bases** are the oxides and hydroxides of metals, with a pH of **greater than 7**. Acids turn litmus **indicator** red and bases turn litmus indicator blue.

Soluble bases (chemicals with a pH greater than 7 and that dissolve in water) are called **alkalis**.

You can find the pH of a solution by using universal indicator. You can add a few drops of universal indicator to the solution and compare the resulting colour against a **pH colour chart**.

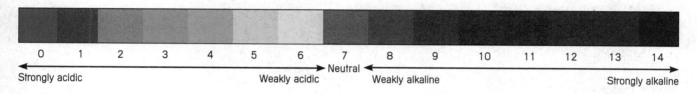

0   1   2   3   4   5   6   7   8   9   10   11   12   13   14

Neutral

Strongly acidic   Weakly acidic   Weakly alkaline   Strongly alkaline

Neutralisation

Metal oxides and metal hydroxides are bases. When they are added to acids in the correct amounts, they can cancel each other out. This is called **neutralisation** because the resulting solution has a **neutral** pH of 7.

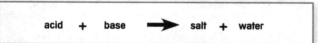

acid + base ⟶ salt + water

As an **acid** is added to an **alkali**, the **pH** of the solution **decreases** because the acid neutralises the alkali to reach pH 7.

As an **alkali** is added to an **acid**, the **pH** of the solution **increases** because the alkali neutralises the acid to reach pH 7.

Acids can also be neutralised by **carbonates** to produce a **salt**, water and carbon dioxide gas.

acid + carbonate ⟶ salt + water + carbon dioxide

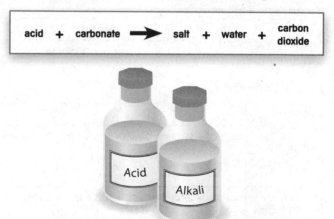

Naming Salts

The **first name** of a salt comes from the name of the **base or carbonate** used, for example:
- **sodium** hydroxide will make a **sodium** salt
- **copper** oxide will make a **copper** salt
- **calcium** carbonate will make a **calcium** salt
- **ammonia** will make an **ammonium** salt.

The **second name** of the salt comes from the **acid** used, for example:
- hydro**chlor**ic acid will produce a **chlor**ide salt
- **sulf**uric acid will produce a **sulf**ate salt
- **nitr**ic acid will produce a **nitr**ate salt
- **phosph**oric acid will produce a **phosph**ate salt.

For example, neutralising **potassium** hydroxide with **nitric** acid will produce **potassium nitrate**.

C2 Acids and Bases

More on Neutralisation

Alkalis in solution contain **hydroxide ions**, **OH⁻(aq)**.

Acids in solution contain **hydrogen** ions, **H⁺(aq)**.

The pH of a solution is a measure of the concentration of H⁺ ions.

(HT) Neutralisation can be described using the ionic equation:

$$H^+(aq) \ + \ OH^-(aq) \ \longrightarrow \ H_2O(l)$$

(HT) Producing Salts

You should be able to construct any of the following word equations and balanced symbol equations for producing salts.

Acid + Base

	Hydrochloric Acid (HCl)	Sulfuric Acid (H_2SO_4)	Nitric Acid (HNO_3)
Sodium Hydroxide (NaOH)	$NaOH + HCl \rightarrow NaCl + H_2O$	$2NaOH + H_2SO_4 \rightarrow Na_2SO_4 + 2H_2O$	$NaOH + HNO_3 \rightarrow NaNO_3 + H_2O$
Potassium Hydroxide (KOH)	$KOH + HCl \rightarrow KCl + H_2O$	$2KOH + H_2SO_4 \rightarrow K_2SO_4 + 2H_2O$	$KOH + HNO_3 \rightarrow KNO_3 + H_2O$
Copper(II) Oxide (CuO)	$CuO + 2HCl \rightarrow CuCl_2 + H_2O$	$CuO + H_2SO_4 \rightarrow CuSO_4 + H_2O$	$CuO + 2HNO_3 \rightarrow Cu(NO_3)_2 + H_2O$
Ammonia (NH_3)	$NH_3 + HCl \rightarrow NH_4Cl$	$2NH_3 + H_2SO_4 \rightarrow (NH_4)_2SO_4$	$NH_3 + HNO_3 \rightarrow NH_4NO_3$

Acid + Carbonate

	Hydrochloric Acid (HCl)	Sulfuric Acid (H_2SO_4)	Nitric Acid (HNO_3)
Sodium Carbonate (Na_2CO_3)	$Na_2CO_3 + 2HCl \rightarrow 2NaCl + H_2O + CO_2$	$Na_2CO_3 + H_2SO_4 \rightarrow Na_2SO_4 + H_2O + CO_2$	$Na_2CO_3 + 2HNO_3 \rightarrow 2NaNO_3 + H_2O + CO_2$
Calcium Carbonate ($CaCO_3$)	$CaCO_3 + 2HCl \rightarrow CaCl_2 + H_2O + CO_2$	$CaCO_3 + H_2SO_4 \rightarrow CaSO_4 + H_2O + CO_2$	$CaCO_3 + 2HNO_3 \rightarrow Ca(NO_3)_2 + H_2O + CO_2$

Quick Test

1. Which elements are found in ammonia?
2. Describe the conditions for the Haber process.
3. What is a reversible reaction?
4. What is an acid?
5. What is an alkali?
6. Write down the general word equation for the reaction between a metal carbonate and an acid.

Fertilisers

Fertilisers are chemicals that give plants **essential chemical elements** needed for growth. Fertilisers:
- make crops grow faster and bigger
- increase the crop **yield**.

As world populations rise, fertilisers can increase food supply but can also cause problems such as the death of animals in waterways. This is known as **eutrophication**.

The three main essential elements found in fertilisers are **nitrogen (N)**, **phosphorus (P)** and **potassium (K)**. **Urea** can also be used as a fertiliser.

Fertilisers must be **soluble in water** so that they can be taken in by the roots of plants in solution.

HT Fertilisers **increase crop yield** by:
- **replacing essential elements** in the soil that have been used up by a previous crop
- **providing nitrogen** as soluble nitrates which are used by the plant to make protein for growth.

Making Fertilisers

Some fertilisers can be manufactured by **neutralising** an **acid** with an **alkali**:
- **Ammonium sulfate** – neutralise sulfuric acid with ammonia.
- **Ammonium nitrate** – neutralise nitric acid with ammonia.
- **Ammonium phosphate** – neutralise phosphoric acid with ammonia.
- **Potassium nitrate** – neutralise nitric acid with potassium hydroxide.

You should be able to label the apparatus needed to make a fertiliser by neutralisation:
- Burette
- Measuring cylinder
- Filter funnel

HT A fertiliser, e.g. potassium nitrate, can be made by producing a salt from neutralisation:

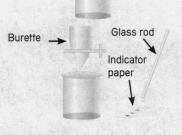

Measuring cylinder

Beaker

Burette

Glass rod

Indicator paper

Evaporating dish

Glass rod

Boiling water

Gauze

Tripod

Bunsen burner

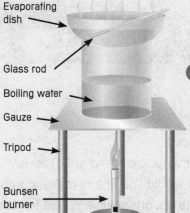

1 Measure out the alkali (e.g. potassium hydroxide) into a beaker using a measuring cylinder.

2 Add acid (e.g. nitric acid) from a burette. Use a glass rod to put a drop of solution onto indicator paper (to test pH). Add the acid a bit at a time until the solution is neutral (pH 7).

3 Transfer the solution to an evaporating dish. Evaporate the solution slowly until crystals form on the end of a cold glass rod. Leave to cool and crystallise.

Eutrophication

Eutrophication is when the overuse of fertilisers changes the ecosystem in lakes, rivers and streams.

HT

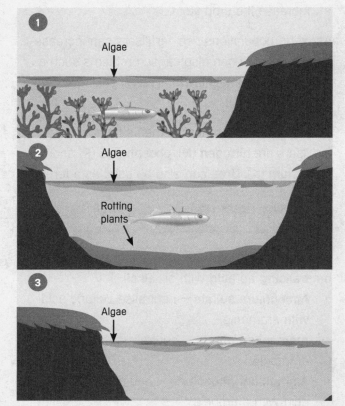

1. Fertilisers used by farmers may be washed into lakes and rivers (run-off). This increases the levels of nitrates and phosphates in the water and more simple algae grow.

2. The algal bloom blocks off sunlight to other plants, causing them to die and rot.

3. Aerobic bacteria feed on the dead organisms and increase in number. They quickly use up the oxygen until nearly all the oxygen is removed. There isn't enough oxygen left to support the larger organisms, such as fish and other aquatic animals, so they suffocate.

Quick Test

1. What is a fertiliser?
2. Which three elements are found in fertilisers?
3. What chemicals would you use to make ammonium sulfate in a neutralisation reaction?
4. **HT** Why do plants absorb soluble nitrate fertiliser?

Sodium Chloride

Sodium chloride, or table salt, is used as a food preservative and flavouring. But it is also useful as a raw material in the chemical industry. It is an important source of chlorine and sodium hydroxide.

Sodium chloride can be removed from the sea or mined from salt deposits. It is mined:
- in Cheshire as a solid (rock salt). This has led to subsidence in some parts of Cheshire
- by solution mining for the chemical industry.

Electrolysis

When concentrated sodium chloride **solution** is electrolysed, the electrodes must be made from **inert** materials as the products are very reactive. This process forms:
- sodium hydroxide in the solution.
- hydrogen at the **cathode** (negative electrode)
- chlorine at the **anode** (positive electrode). You can test for chlorine using damp litmus paper; if chlorine is present, it will bleach the litmus paper.

There are many uses for the products of **electrolysis** of sodium chloride:
- Sodium hydroxide is used to make soap.
- Hydrogen is used in the manufacture of margarine.

- Chlorine is used to sterilise water, make solvents and plastics, for example, PVC.
- Chlorine and sodium hydroxide are reacted together to make household bleach.

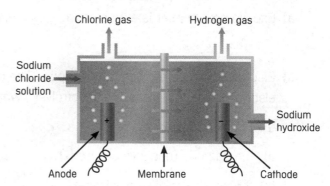

HT Electrolysis of Sodium Chloride

Brine ($NaCl(aq)$) contains Na^+, Cl^-, OH^- and H^+ ions. The large scale electrolysis of brine happens as part of the chloro-alkali industry. This is a global market which generates great profits.

- Hydrogen is made by **reduction** at the cathode:

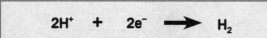

$$2H^+ + 2e^- \longrightarrow H_2$$

Reduction is gain of electrons.

- Chlorine is made by **oxidation** at the anode:

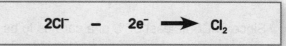

$$2Cl^- - 2e^- \longrightarrow Cl_2$$

Oxidation is loss of electrons.

Sodium (Na^+) and hydroxide (OH^-) ions remain in solution. This makes the third product of sodium hydroxide.

Quick Test

1. What are the three products of the electrolysis of sodium chloride solution?
2. How is household bleach made?
3. What is a use for chlorine?

C2 Exam Practice Questions

1 The Earth is made up of three layers: the crust, the mantle and the core. What is the lithosphere? **[1]**

....

2 Decide whether each of the following building materials is manufactured or natural. **[3]**

Slate ....

Steel ....

Cement ....

Marble ....

Brick ....

3 Copper is an important metal found in ores.

   a) Explain how copper is extracted from its ore. **[1]**

....

   b) Electrical wires are made out of copper. The copper needs to be very pure. Copper is purified by electrolysis. In the process of electrolysis, what is:

      i) the electrolyte? ....

      ii) the cathode (negative electrode)? ....

      iii) the anode (positive electrode)? .... **[3]**

4 Iron in the form of steel is often used to make car bodies. What two substances must be present to make iron rust? **[2]**

....

5 Since 2006 at least 85% of a car has to be able to be recycled.

What are the two main environmental reasons for recycling a car at the end of its useful life? **[2]**

....

....

6 Fertilisers are used by many farmers across the UK.

   a) Why do farmers add fertilisers to their soil? **[1]**

....

   b) Explain how a fertiliser works. **[2]**

....

7 The Haber process is used in industry to make ammonia (NH_3). The graph on the right shows how the yield changes with temperature and pressure.

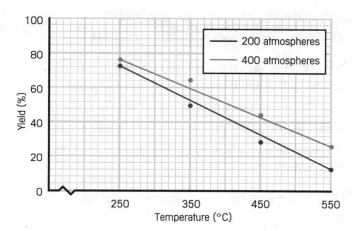

a) Name the two reactants used for making ammonia. **[1]**

b) What is the yield of ammonia when the temperature is 250°C and the pressure is 200 atmospheres? **[1]**

c) At what temperature was the yield 44% when the pressure was 400 atmospheres? **[1]**

d) If the temperature was 250°C, which pressure would give the greatest yield? **[1]**

e) Explain what happens to the yield as temperature increases. **[1]**

8 Ammonium nitrate is an example of a fertiliser that can be made from a neutralisation reaction.

a) What alkali would be reacted with nitric acid to make this fertiliser? **[1]**

HT

b) Write a balanced symbol equation for this reaction. **[3]**

9 The crust of the Earth is split into large pieces of rock known as tectonic plates.

There are different types of plate boundaries where the plates meet.

What happens at a subduction zone? **[3]**

P1 Heating Houses

Temperature

Temperature is a measure of how **hot** something is. The unit of measurement is degrees Celsius (°C). Temperature can be represented by a range of colours in a **thermogram**. Hottest areas appear white/yellow/red; coldest areas appear black/dark blue/purple.

Heat is a measurement of **energy** and is measured in joules (J).

(HT) **Temperature** is a measurement of how hot something is using an arbitrary or **chosen scale**, usually degrees Celsius, Kelvin or sometimes degrees Fahrenheit (°F).

The temperature of an object is a measurement of the average kinetic energy of the particles in that object.

Heat is a measurement of energy on an **absolute scale**, always joules.

In this thermogram:
- the windows are where most heat energy is escaping — they show up as yellow
- the well-insulated loft is where the least heat energy is escaping — it shows up as purple.

Temperature Change

If there is a **difference** in temperature between an **object** and its **surroundings**, then **heat energy flows** from the hotter region to the cooler region.
- If an object's **temperature rises**, it is **taking in** heat energy. For example, if you take a can of cola out of the fridge it will soon warm up to room temperature, or **ambient temperature**, because the can takes in heat energy from the air in the room.
- If an object's **temperature falls**, it is **giving out** heat energy. For example, a hot cup of tea will cool down until it reaches room temperature. If you hold it in your hands you'll feel the heat energy flowing from the cup into your hands.

An object that has a very high temperature will cool down very quickly. As its temperature drops, it will cool down at a slower rate.

The rate of heating or cooling depends on the difference between the temperature of the object and the ambient temperature around it. The greater the difference, the greater the rate (and the steeper the curve on the graph).

Graph to show Temperature of a Cup of Tea

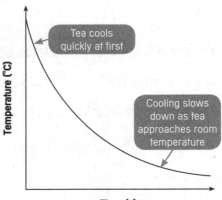

Tea cools quickly at first

Cooling slows down as tea approaches room temperature

Temperature (°C)

Time (s)

Degrees Celsius • Thermogram • Joule

Measuring Heat Energy

The amount of **energy** needed to raise the temperature of an object depends on:

- the **mass** of the object
- the **change** in temperature **required**
- the **material** it's made from.

The equipment shown alongside can be used to measure the amount of heat energy required to change the temperature of an aluminium block.

This 100W electric heater provides 100J of heat energy per second, i.e. 100J of heat energy passes into the aluminium every second.

Time how many seconds it takes for the temperature of the aluminium to rise by a certain amount, e.g. 10°C. You can then calculate the amount of energy used to bring about the change using this formula:

| Total energy supplied | = | Energy supplied per second | × | Number of seconds |

Example

It takes the heater 50 seconds to raise the temperature of the aluminium block by 10°C. Calculate the total energy supplied. Remember, the heater transfers 100J of heat energy per second.

$$\text{Total energy supplied} = \text{Energy supplied per second} \times \text{Number of seconds}$$
$$= 100\text{J/s} \times 50\text{s} = \textbf{5000J}$$

Thermometer

Power supply

Insulation   Electric heater   Aluminium block

The electric heater is known as the heat **source**.
The aluminium block is the heat **sink**.

Specific Heat Capacity

Each material has a value of how much energy it can hold. This is known as **specific heat capacity**.

Specific heat capacity is the energy needed to raise the temperature of 1kg of material by 1°C.

The following equation is used to find the amount of energy required to raise the temperature of an object by a certain amount.

| Energy (J) | = | Mass (kg) | × | Specific heat capacity (J/kg°C) | × | Temperature change (°C) |

(HT) You may be required to rearrange this equation to do a calculation.

Example

It takes 28 800J of heat energy to raise the temperature of a 4kg block of aluminium by 8°C. Calculate the specific heat capacity of aluminium.

$$\text{Specific heat capacity} = \frac{\text{Energy}}{\text{Mass} \times \text{Temperature change}}$$

$$= \frac{28\,800\text{J}}{4\text{kg} \times 8°\text{C}} = \textbf{900J/kg°C}$$

Melting and Boiling

Energy is needed to **melt** or **boil** substances. This is why the temperature of a material **doesn't change** when it's at the point of boiling, melting or freezing (i.e. **changing state**).

For example, the graph below shows how the temperature of a block of ice changes as it's heated up:

① The temperature rises sharply to begin with.

② Once it hits 0°C, it stops rising. This is because all the energy is being used to change the state of the ice from solid to liquid. The temperature stays at 0°C until **all** of the ice has melted.

③ The temperature rises until it reaches 100°C.

④ The temperature remains constant again, while the water changes state from liquid to gas (steam).

The temperature of water will never rise above 100°C, no matter how long it is heated for. But, the temperature of the gas (steam) produced from it can rise.

So, to interpret data that shows the heating or cooling of an object, look for places where the temperature stays the same.

(HT) During the melting and boiling of water, the energy supplied is used to **break intermolecular bonds** as the water molecules change state from solid to liquid, and from liquid to gas. This explains why the temperature of the material doesn't change.

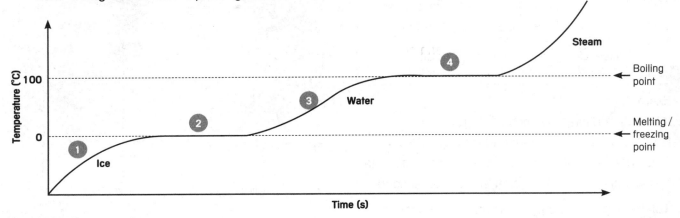

Specific Latent Heat

The amount of heat energy required to melt or boil 1kg of a material is called the **specific latent heat**.

It depends on:

- the **material**
- the **state** (solid, liquid or gas).

The energy required to boil or melt a certain mass of a material can be found using this equation:

Energy (J) = Mass (kg) × Specific latent heat (J/kg)

Example

An ice sculpture with a mass of 10kg is left to melt on a hot day. The specific latent heat of ice is 330 000J/kg. Calculate the amount of energy required to melt the ice.

Energy = Mass × Specific latent heat
= 10kg × 330 000J/kg = **3 300 000J**

Quick Test

① State the units of temperature and heat energy.

② On a thermogram of two objects, one appears blue in colour and the other one is yellow. Which object is giving out the most heat energy?

Conductors and Insulators

Materials that allow energy to flow through them quickly are called **conductors**. Metals are good conductors.

Materials that allow energy to flow through them much more slowly are called **insulators**. Most non-metals, such as wood, plastic, glass and air are good insulators.

Curtains are good insulators because they **trap a layer of air** between them and the window, which helps reduce energy loss. Air is a good insulator because the particles are very far apart.

Saving Energy in the Home

Design features in the home help to **save energy** by reducing heat loss by **conduction**, **convection** and **radiation**. This table explains how.

Method of Insulation	Reduces:	How?
Fibreglass (or mineral wool) roof insulation	Conduction and convection	By trapping layers of air (a very good insulator) between the fibres.
Reflective foil on walls	Radiation	By reflecting heat energy back into the room.
Foam cavity wall insulation	Conduction and convection	By trapping air in the foam. (The air is an insulator and prevents conduction; being trapped stops it moving and so prevents convection.)
Double glazing	Conduction and convection	By trapping air between the panes of glass.
Draught excluders	Conduction and convection	By keeping as much warm air inside as possible.

Reducing Heat Loss in the Home

There are many different ways in which heat loss from a home can be **reduced**. Many insulation materials contain air, which is a very good insulator.

$$\text{Payback time (in years)} = \frac{\text{Cost of installing insulation}}{\text{Annual saving}}$$

Method of Insulation	Cost	Annual Saving	Payback Time
Fibreglass roof insulation	£400	£80	5 years
Reflective foil on or in walls	£40	£10	4 years
Cavity wall insulation	£600	£30	20 years
Double glazing	£1800	£60	30 years
Draught excluders	£40	£20	2 years

An important consideration with each method is the **payback time**, i.e. how long it takes to pay for the insulation from the savings made.

P1 Keeping Homes Warm

HT Cavity Wall Insulation

A **cavity wall** is made up of an inner and an outer wall separated by a cavity (space) filled with air. Trapped air is a good insulator, but in the cavity it is free to move.

The heat energy passes through the wall (from the radiator) by **conduction**. This heats the air in the cavity. The heat is then carried away from the wall by **convection**. Heat loss can be significantly reduced by filling the cavity with foam. The foam contains trapped air (a good insulator) so heat loss by conduction is reduced. The air is trapped in the foam, so heat loss by convection is reduced.

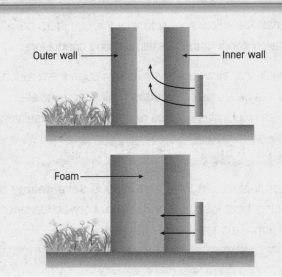

Energy Efficiency

Energy efficiency is a measure of how good an appliance is at **converting** input energy into **useful** output energy.

For example, the input energy for a television is electrical energy and the useful output energy is light and sound. But a television also produces heat energy, which is **wasted** energy, i.e. it isn't needed.

You can use this equation to calculate efficiency:

$$\text{Efficiency} = \frac{\text{Useful output energy (J)}}{\text{Total input energy (J)}} \times 100$$

Example
A 60 watt light bulb **uses** 60 joules of energy every second. Each second it **gives out** 6 joules of light energy. What is the efficiency of the light bulb?

$$\text{Efficiency} = \frac{\text{Useful output energy}}{\text{Total energy input}} \times 100$$

$$= \frac{6J}{60J} \times 100$$

$$= 0.1 \times 100 = \textbf{10\%}$$

This **Sankey diagram** shows the efficiency of a different light bulb.

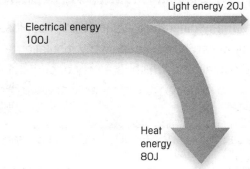

$$\text{Efficiency} = \frac{20J}{100J} \times 100 = 20\% \text{ efficient}$$

Transfer of Heat Energy

Air is a good **insulator**, because the particles are far apart. If air is trapped in a material, the material will be an insulator.

Heat energy doesn't stay in one place; it moves around. Hot air rises and is replaced by colder air. Heat energy can be transferred from one place to another by **conduction**, **convection** or **radiation**.

Efficiency • Conduction • Convection • Radiation

Transfer of Heat Energy (Cont.)

Here are some examples of how energy transfers are reduced in everyday situations:

- Kettles made of metal have shiny surfaces to reduce heat loss by radiation.

- Hot-water tanks are made of stainless steel and may also have a shiny outer layer to reduce heat loss by radiation. Hot-water tanks also usually have an insulating jacket to reduce heat loss by conduction and convection.

Conduction

Conduction is the transfer of heat energy **through a substance** from a hotter region to a cooler region without any movement of the substance itself.

(HT) As a substance, e.g. a metal poker, is heated, the kinetic energy of the particles increases. This kinetic energy is transferred between the particles and energy is transferred along the substance.

Metals have free electrons which can move through the material carrying energy. This makes metals very good conductors.

Transfer of Heat from Hotter to Cooler Region

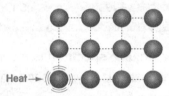

Heat →

Quick Test

1. Which type of house insulation has the longest payback time?
2. Name the useful energies produced by a television.

Convection

Convection is the transfer of heat energy from hotter regions to cooler regions by the **movement of particles**.

(HT) As a liquid or gas gets hotter, its particles move faster, causing it to expand and become less dense. The particles in the hotter region will rise up and be replaced by particles from the colder, denser region.

Circulation of Air Caused by a Radiator

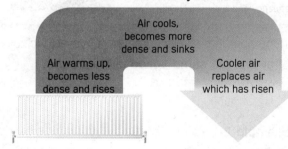

Air cools, becomes more dense and sinks

Air warms up, becomes less dense and rises

Cooler air replaces air which has risen

Radiation

Hot objects **emit** mainly **infra-red radiation**, an electromagnetic wave, which can pass through a vacuum, i.e. no medium is needed for its transfer. The amount of radiation given out or taken in by an object depends on its surface.

Dark matt surfaces emit more radiation than light shiny surfaces **at the same temperature**. Dark matt surfaces are better absorbers (poorer reflectors) of radiation than light shiny surfaces at the same temperature.

P1 A Spectrum of Waves

Light

Light is a **transverse wave**. A transverse wave has the following features:

- **Amplitude** – the maximum disturbance caused by the wave.
- **Wavelength** – the distance between corresponding points on two successive disturbances (e.g. from one crest to the next crest).
- **Frequency** – the number of waves produced (or that pass a particular point) in one second.

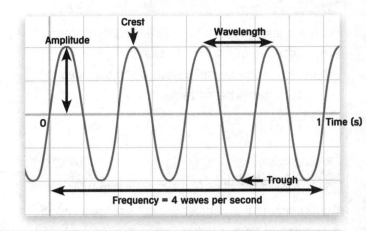

The Electromagnetic Spectrum

The **electromagnetic spectrum** is a continuous spectrum that extends beyond each end of the visible spectrum for light.

It includes **microwaves** and **infrared radiation**.

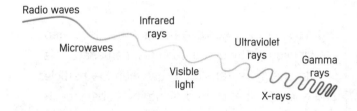

Radio waves
Microwaves
Infrared rays
Visible light
Ultraviolet rays
X-rays
Gamma rays

The Wave Equation

You can calculate the **speed** of a wave using this equation:

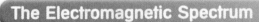

Wave speed (m/s) = Frequency (Hz) × Wavelength (m)

$$\frac{v}{f \times \lambda}$$

where v is wave speed, f is frequency and λ is wavelength.

But remember that all electromagnetic waves, including light, travel at the **same speed** in a **vacuum** (e.g. space).

Example 1

A tapped tuning fork with a frequency of 480Hz produces sound waves of wavelength 70cm. What is the speed of the sound wave?

Wave speed = Frequency × Wavelength
= 480Hz × 0.7m
= **336m/s**

Remember to calculate using the correct units

(HT) Example 2

Radio 5 Live transmits on a frequency of 909kHz. If the speed of radio waves is 300 000 000m/s, on what wavelength does it transmit?

$$\text{Wavelength} = \frac{\text{Wave speed}}{\text{Frequency}}$$

$$= \frac{300\,000\,000\text{m/s}}{909\,000\text{Hz}}$$

$$= \textbf{330m}$$

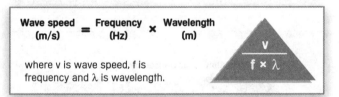

Reflection

Light or another electromagnetic wave can be **reflected** from multiple surfaces, as shown in the diagram.

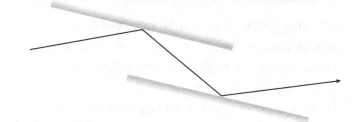

Refraction

A wave will speed up or slow down as it passes from one medium (material) into another. This can cause the wave to change direction and is known as **refraction**.

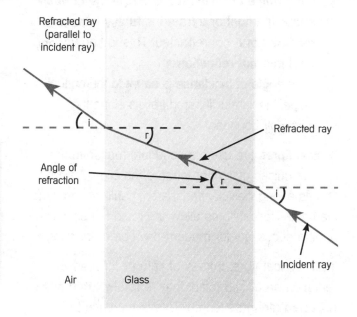

Refracted ray (parallel to incident ray)

Refracted ray

Angle of refraction

Incident ray

Air   Glass

Quick Test

1. What is meant by the 'frequency of a wave'?
2. Name two electromagnetic waves with a shorter wavelength than visible light.
3. (HT) State the condition needed for maximum diffraction.

Diffraction

As waves pass through a gap or an opening (such as a door), the edges spread out. This is **diffraction**.

Gap larger than wavelength – slight diffraction

(HT) Maximum diffraction occurs when the gap is the same width as the wavelength of the wave passing through it. This phenomenon limits the resolution and quality of the image produced by telescopes and optical microscopes. As light passes between two neighbouring particles, it is diffracted.

The intensity of the image is reduced. The light may also interfere with other diffracted light waves, distorting the image further.

Gap same size as wavelength – increased diffraction

P1 Light and Lasers

Reflection and Refraction

Light and infrared rays can be **reflected** or **refracted** when they cross a glass–air boundary. It depends on the **angle of incidence** (the angle at which they hit the boundary):

1 If the **angle of incidence** is **below** the critical angle, the light or infrared is **refracted** away from the normal.

2 If the **angle of incidence** is **above** the **critical angle**, the light or infrared is totally internally reflected and not refracted. This is known as **total internal reflection**.

3 If the **angle of incidence** is **equal to** the **critical angle**, the light or infrared travels along the glass–air boundary.

Optical fibres are used to send information in the form of pulses of light or infrared radiation. An optical fibre is a long, flexible, transparent cable of very small diameter. Optical fibres allow the rapid transmission of data necessary for modern-day communications.

In an optical fibre, **pulses** of light or infrared radiation aren't refracted: they're **totally internally reflected** along its length. This is because the glass–air boundary acts like a plane mirror.

Total internal reflection also occurs at water–air and Perspex–air boundaries.

Light is transmitted down a fibre optic cable by total internal reflection.

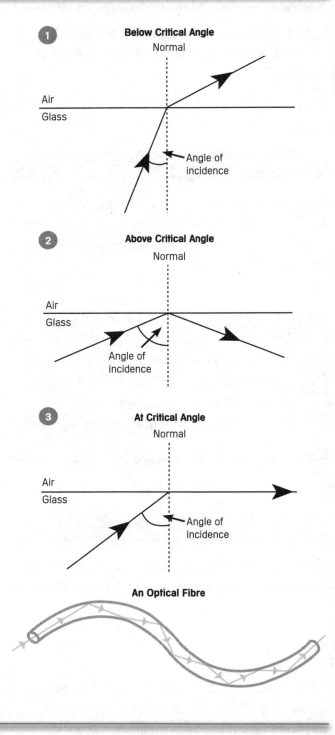

1 Below Critical Angle
Normal
Air
Glass
Angle of incidence

2 Above Critical Angle
Normal
Air
Glass
Angle of incidence

3 At Critical Angle
Normal
Air
Glass
Angle of incidence

An Optical Fibre

Wireless Signals

Electromagnetic radiation (e.g. microwaves) can be used to **send information** without optical fibres because it can be **reflected** and **refracted** in the same way as visible light. This is why it is known as **wireless technology**.

Wireless technology is used in radios, mobile phones and laptop computers. It has three main advantages:
- Signals are available 24 hours a day.
- No wiring is needed.
- Items can be portable and convenient.

Communication Signals

At the beginning of the last century, **Morse code** was used to communicate over long distances. This code uses long and short flashes of light to represent letters.

Like all electromagnetic waves, light travels very fast. This is why modern technology uses light as its signal.

Light used for communication is produced by a **laser**. A laser produces a narrow, intense beam of light.

Optical fibres are used to carry signals in **binary code** (digital signals).

(HT) This table lists the advantages and disadvantages of using various signals to send information:

Signal	Advantages	Disadvantages
Light	• Travels very fast • Small loss of signal	• Can't be used for wireless signalling as it doesn't diffract well
Electrical	• Can be sent along wires	• Signal deteriorates
Radio waves	• Can be used for wireless signalling as the waves can diffract around obstacles	• Diffraction leads to signal loss

Morse code is a digital signal because the light is either **on** or **off**.

Lasers

A **laser** produces a narrow beam of monochromatic (single colour) light.

Some uses of lasers include surgery and dental treatment, cutting materials in industry, weapon guidance and laser light shows.

(HT) **Lasers** produce a beam of light in which all light waves:
- have the same frequency
- are **in phase** with each other
- have low divergence.

Example

1. The bottom surface of a CD contains billions of tiny bumps (called pits).
2. The pits store information digitally.
3. When a CD spins, laser light is reflected by the pits.
4. The reflected pulses of light are turned into electrical signals on their way to the amplifier.

'**In phase**' means all the peaks and troughs match up, i.e. they go up together and down together:
- Waves **in phase** transfer a lot of energy.
- Waves **out of phase** transfer less overall energy.

Waves in Phase

Waves out of Phase

Electromagnetic Radiation

The amount of radiation (such as infrared) that is absorbed or emitted from a surface depends on:

- surface temperature
- colour – black is good, white and silver are poor
- texture – dull is good, shiny is poor.

Uses of Electromagnetic Radiation

Electromagnetic radiations have many uses.

Microwaves are used to heat materials, as well as for satellite communication, mobile phones and radar. They:

- are **absorbed** by water and fat molecules, which causes them to heat up
- can **penetrate** about 1cm into food
- can cause burns when absorbed by body tissue
- can **travel** through glass and plastics
- are reflected by shiny metal surfaces.

Infrared rays are used to heat materials (in cooking), and in remote controls. They are:

- used to **heat** the surface of the food in cooking
- **reflected** off shiny surfaces
- **absorbed** by black objects.

HT Transferring Energy

Microwaves and infrared energy are transferred to materials in different ways.

Microwaves are absorbed by water and fat molecules in the outside layers of the food, increasing the kinetic energy of the particles. Energy is then transferred to the centre of the food by **conduction** or **convection**.

Infrared is absorbed by all of the particles on the surface of the food, increasing the kinetic energy of the particles. Energy is then transferred to the centre of the food by **conduction** or **convection**.

The amount of energy a microwave or an infrared wave has depends on its frequency, and this determines how potentially dangerous it could be.

Microwaves

Microwaves are used to **transmit information** over large distances that are in **line of sight**. Some areas aren't in line of sight so they have **poor signals**, which is why your mobile phone may cut out or fail to get a connection in certain areas.

The microwave signals that mobile phones use aren't the same wavelength as the microwaves used in microwave ovens.

Microwaves (Cont.)

There are some concerns that microwaves emitted by mobile phones could have a **harmful effect**. For example, microwaves *could* cause ear or brain tumours, brain damage or changes to DNA.

If using mobile phones affects people's health, then children could be more at risk from the microwave signals because their skulls are very thin. The potential risk is increased if the mobile phone is used more frequently.

There is also public concern about mobile phone transmission masts and the possible dangers to people who live near them.

Scientists publish studies into the effects of microwave radiation from mobile phones and mobile phone transmission masts. This enables other scientists to share their studies and check data from other studies.

(HT) Sometimes scientists publish conflicting evidence about studies such as mobile phone safety. In such cases, society must make choices (by balancing risk and benefit) about their own mobile phone use and/or whether to live near to a mobile phone mast.

Microwave Signals

Microwave signals can be lost or affected by:
- large obstacles such as trees or mountains, which block the signal. Microwaves are not diffracted around large objects
- poor weather conditions and large areas of surface water
- the curvature of the Earth
- **interference** between signals.

Some of the problems can be reduced by:
- limiting the distance between transmitters
- positioning masts high on top of hills and/or tall buildings.

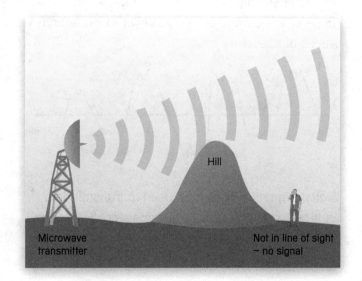

Microwave transmitter

Hill

Not in line of sight – no signal

Quick Test

1. Other than heating food, state two uses of microwaves.
2. What type of molecules in foods absorb microwaves?
3. What happens to light when it hits a glass–air boundary at an angle above the critical angle of substance?

P1 Data Transmission

Infrared Signals

Infrared radiation is a type of electromagnetic wave.

Infrared is used in many commonplace devices, for example:

- remote controls for your television and video
- sensors that control automatic doors in shops
- short-distance wireless data links for computers or mobile phones
- burglar alarms (by detecting body heat)
- security lights (by detecting body heat).

The infrared signal from a TV remote control uses digital codes to control the different functions of the TV. Each function has a different code. When a button is pressed the code is transmitted to the TV as a series of flashes.

An example of these codes might be:

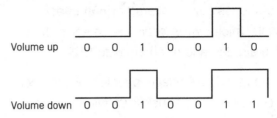

Volume up   0   0   1   0   0   1   0

Volume down   0   0   1   0   0   1   1

Analogue and Digital Signals

Analogue signals can be used to transmit data. They **vary continuously** in **amplitude**.

Analogue signals can have **any value** within a fixed range of values and are very similar to the sound waves of speech or music.

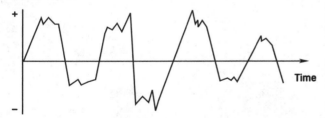

Digital signals can also be used to transmit data as a series of **pulses**. Digital signals don't vary; they only have **two states** – on (1) and off (0). There are no values in between.

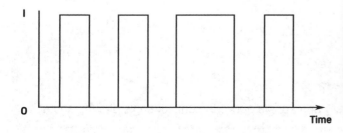

(HT) Two or more digital signals can be sent down the same **optical fibre** at the same time. This enables more information to be sent in one go, and is known as multiplexing.

Both digital and analogue signals suffer from **interference** in the form of noise. But interference doesn't affect digital signals because the signal is still only on or off. The information is in the pulse pattern (length of the on and off sections).

Analogue Signal – poor signal quality due to interference

Digital Signal – high signal quality as interference is easily removed

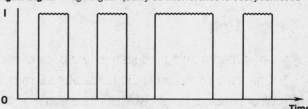

Radiation for Communication

Radiation used for communication can be reflected by the atmosphere. This allows broadcasts from the south coast of England to be received in France (around the curve of the Earth). Radio stations and other nearby broadcasters must transmit using different **frequencies** to avoid interference.

Wireless technology is used for TV and radio broadcasts, mobile phones and laptops (wireless internet). Advantages and disadvantages of wireless communication are shown in the table.

Advantages
• No connection to a phone land-line required.
• Portable, convenient, allows access anywhere.
Disadvantage
• Aerial is needed to pick up the signal.

HT Transmitting Signals

Satellites can be used for **global communication**. A signal is sent from a ground station transmitter dish to a satellite receiver dish. A return signal is then sent by the satellite transmitter to a ground receiver dish, which may be in a different country, continent, etc.

The **ionosphere** is an electrically charged layer in the Earth's upper atmosphere. Longer wavelength radio waves are **reflected** by the ionosphere. This enables radio and television programmes to be transmitted between different places.

The **refraction** and **diffraction** of radiation, e.g. microwaves, can affect communications.

Refraction at the interfaces of different layers of the Earth's atmosphere results in the waves **changing direction**. Diffraction (changes to the direction and intensity of waves) at the edge of transmission dishes causes the waves to **spread out**, which results in **signal loss**.

Interference from similar signals limits the distance between transmitters. Positioning transmitters in high places can help to overcome the nuisance of obstacles blocking signals.

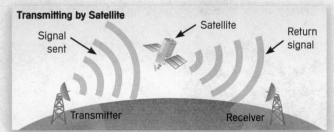

Transmitting by Satellite
Signal sent — Satellite — Return signal — Transmitter — Receiver

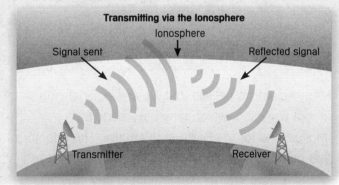

Transmitting via the Ionosphere
Signal sent — Ionosphere — Reflected signal — Transmitter — Receiver

DAB Radio

New DAB (Digital Audio Broadcasting) radios receive digital signals.

Most are also able to receive old FM radio station signals which are transmitted using analogue signals.

Advantages of DAB
• More stations are available.
• Less interference with broadcasts from other stations.
Disadvantages of DAB
• Audio quality is not as good as FM broadcasts.
• Some areas cannot receive DAB (e.g. the short wavelength signal cannot diffract around hills.

Earthquakes

Earthquakes produce **shock waves**, which can travel inside the Earth. They can damage buildings and cause tsunamis. These waves are called seismic waves and can be detected by **seismometers**.

There are two main types of seismic wave – **P-waves** and **S-waves**.

P-waves (primary waves) are longitudinal and travel through both solids and liquids.

S-waves (secondary waves) are transverse waves and travel through solids but not through liquids. They travel more **slowly** than P-waves.

(HT) Detecting Seismic Waves

After an earthquake occurs, the waves are **detected** all over the world, as shown in the diagram.

P-waves are detected in most places, so this means they can travel through the solid **crust** and **mantle**, and the liquid **outer core** and the **inner core**.

S-waves are only detected closer to the **epicentre** (the centre of the earthquake). This means they can pass through the solid **crust** and **mantle**, but they **can't** pass through the liquid outer core.

So, the properties of seismic waves provide evidence for the structure of the Earth.

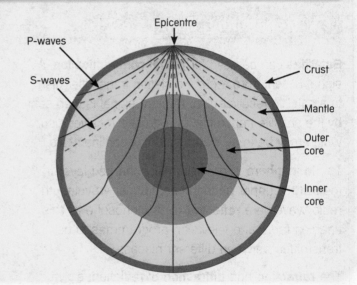

Global Warming

Many scientists believe that we are experiencing global warming, which may have serious implications for the Earth in the future. Three factors that contribute to global warming are:

- increased **energy** use in homes and industry
- increased **carbon dioxide** (CO_2) **emissions** from fossil fuels
- deforestation (the cutting down of large numbers of trees).

Weather patterns are affected by human activity, as well as by natural phenomena, for example:

- dust from volcanoes reflects radiation from the Sun back into space, causing **cooling**.
- dust from factories reflects radiation from cities back towards the Earth, causing **warming**.

Quick Test

1. Which type of seismic wave cannot travel through the liquid outer core of the Earth?
2. Deforestation contributes to global warming. True or false?

Dangerous Sun

The Sun produces **electromagnetic waves**, including **ultraviolet** radiation. Prolonged exposure to ultraviolet radiation can cause a sun tan, sun burn, cataracts, premature ageing and skin cancer.

Sunscreen can be effective at **reducing** the **damage** caused by ultraviolet radiation. The higher the **factor**, the lower the **risk** because high factors allow longer exposure without burning. On a bright, sunny day in England you should spend no more than 20 minutes in the sun without sun protection. The factor of sunscreen you put on increases the amount of time you can safely stay in the sun for, e.g. wearing a factor 30 sunscreen means you can stay in the sun for 30 times longer than if you had no sunscreen on: 20 mins × 30 = 600 mins = **10 hours**. But you must keep reapplying it!

People who have darker skin tones have a reduced risk of developing skin cancer. Skin cancer develops in the delicate tissues below the melanin in the skin. Melanin is the chemical which gives skin its colour. Dark skin absorbs more ultraviolet radiation than light skin. Less ultraviolet radiation reaches the underlying body tissues.

Public health campaigns have informed people about the risks of ultraviolet rays. They use a range of media in the campaigns: TV adverts, leaflets, newspapers, internet campaigns.

To reduce the risk of sunburn and developing skin cancer:
- stay out of the midday sun
- keep skin covered (wear long sleeves and a hat)
- reduce or avoid use of sun beds
- always use sun block or sunscreen.

The Ozone Layer

(HT) Ozone is a gas found naturally high up in the Earth's **atmosphere**, which **prevents** too many harmful **ultraviolet** (UV) rays reaching the Earth.

Recently, scientists have noticed a link between the decreasing thickness of the ozone layer and the number of people suffering from skin cancer.

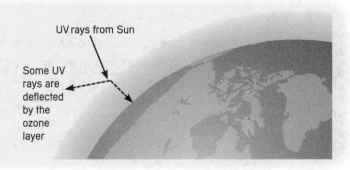

UV rays from Sun

Some UV rays are deflected by the ozone layer

Scientists who study the ozone layer must make sure their data is accurate. In order to do so, they:
- repeat their experiments using new equipment
- consider data from other scientists who replicated their experiments
- test their predictions based on current explanations.

(HT) The discovery of the hole in the ozone layer over Antarctica had an impact globally:
- Legislation was passed in many countries to ban the use of CFCs in fridge cooling systems.
- Old fridges and freezers containing CFCs must be disposed of according to strict guidelines.
- CFCs are no longer used as propellants in aerosol cans (e.g. hairspray and deodorant).

The discovery also raised a greater awareness of the risk of ultraviolet radiation and its link to sun burn and skin cancer.

P1 Exam Practice Questions

1. Naz eats an ice cream in the sun. The graph shows the change in temperature of the ice cream.

   a) Explain what is happening at point B. **[1]**

   ....

   ....

   b) Explain what is meant by **specific heat capacity.** **[1]**

   ....

   c) The mass of Naz's ice cream is 63g and the specific heat capacity is 1.67kJ/kg°C. Use this information and the graph above to calculate the energy transferred to the ice cream before point A. **[2]**

   ....

   ....

2. Calculate the efficiency of a light bulb that uses 100 joules of energy every second to produce 20 joules of light energy. **[2]**

   ....

   ....

3. Claire has bought a new microwave oven as she finds microwaves easy to use and convenient for cooking. Briefly explain how microwaves are used to heat food. **[4]**

   ....

   ....

   ....

4. Name the parts of the wave labelled on the diagram. **[4]**

   A ....

   B ....

   C ....

   D ....

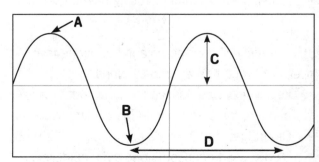

5 A radio station transmits at a frequency of 890 000Hz. The wavelength of the wave is 337m. Calculate the speed of the electromagnetic wave. **[2]**

6 a) What are the two main types of seismic wave called? **[1]**

b) Which of the waves named in part (a) cannot pass through the liquid part of the core? **[1]**

7 Bartez starts to burn if he stays out in the sun for 6 minutes. He applies a sun cream with SPF 20 Calculate how long he can now stay in the sun for before burning. **[2]**

8 John wants to insulate his house. He has gathered data about the different types of domestic insulation available, shown in the table.

a) Fill in the spaces in the 'Payback Time' column. **[3]**

Insulation Type	Cost	Annual Saving	Payback Time
Cavity Wall Insulation	£500	£25	
Double Glazing	£2100	£70	
Draft Excluders	£30	£20	

b) Using the data in the table, suggest which type of insulation John should choose. Explain your answer. **[1]**

(HT) c) John puts shiny foil behind the radiators in his house. Explain how this helps to reduce his energy bills. **[4]**

P2 Collecting Energy from the Sun

Energy from the Sun

The Sun is a stable **source** of energy. It emits and transfers energy to Earth as **light** and **heat**. Energy from the Sun can be captured and used to produce **electricity** and heat.

Energy from the Sun is known as **renewable** energy because it will not run out.

Photocells

Photocells capture light energy from the Sun on flat silicon surfaces. The light energy is then **transformed** into an **electric current** which travels in the same direction all the time. This type of electric current is known as **direct current** (**DC**).

The **power** output of a photocell depends on the surface **area** exposed to the sunlight. Lots of photocells can be joined together (as a **solar panel**) to create a larger surface area. This increases the amount of light captured from the Sun.

Some advantages and disadvantages of photocells are listed in this table.

Advantages

- They use renewable energy from the Sun.
- No need for fuel (the Sun is the energy source).
- No pollution or waste is produced.
- Little maintenance is required once they are installed.
- Have a long life.
- Can operate in remote locations to give access to electricity without installing power cables.

Disadvantages

- No power at night or during bad weather.
- Expensive to buy.
- Take up a lot of space.

HT How Photocells Work

The Sun's energy is **absorbed** by the photocell, causing **electrons** to be knocked loose from the silicon atoms in the crystal. These electrons **flow** freely within the silicon. This flow of charge is called an **electric current**.

The **power** of a photocell depends on:
- the **surface area** exposed to the light
- the **intensity** of the **light** (intensity is a measure of how powerful the light energy is)
- the distance between the light source and the photocell.

To maximise power output, an efficient solar collector must **track** (follow) the position of the Sun in the sky. This requires additional technology, which increases the initial set-up cost.

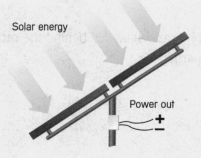

Solar energy

Power out

Other Uses of the Sun's Energy

Light from the Sun can be captured and used in other ways, apart from in photocells.

Light can be **absorbed** by a surface and transformed into heat energy. Water passes over this surface to be **heated** to a reasonable temperature. It can then be used to heat buildings.

A curved mirror can be used to **focus** the Sun's light, rather like a magnifying glass, making it more **intense**.

Buildings with a large number of windows facing the Sun can be heated by **passive solar heating**. Passive solar heating refers to a device (e.g. a greenhouse) that traps energy from the Sun but doesn't distribute the energy or change it into another form of energy. Passive solar heating causes conservatories to get hot in the summer.

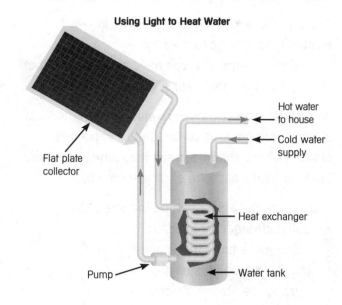

Using Light to Heat Water

Flat plate collector

Hot water to house

Cold water supply

Heat exchanger

Pump

Water tank

(HT) Glass is transparent to radiation from the Sun. Passive solar heating is caused by visible light and infrared radiation passing through glass into a room. The light and infrared is **absorbed** by objects in the room, causing them to **heat up**. The objects then re-emit infrared of longer wavelength, which can't pass back through glass. Instead, it is **reflected** back into the room, causing the room to heat up.

Wind Turbines

The Sun's energy also produces **convection currents** in the air (i.e. wind). Wind turbines transform the kinetic energy of the air into **electrical energy**.

The advantages and disadvantages of wind turbines are listed in this table:

Advantages
• Wind is a renewable energy source.
• There is no chemical pollution or waste.
• It is free – after set-up costs.

Disadvantages
• Turbines require a large amount of space to deliver a reasonable amount of electricity.
• They are dependent on the wind (unreliable).
• Turbines cause visual pollution.

P2 Generating Electricity

The Dynamo Effect

The **dynamo effect** refers to the way in which **electricity** can be generated by:

- moving a **wire**, or a coil of wire, near a **magnet**
- moving a magnet near a wire, or coil of wire.

When this happens, the wire cuts through the lines of force of the **magnetic field** and a **current** is **produced** by **electromagnetic induction** in the wire (as long as it's part of a complete **circuit**).

The current generated can be **increased** by:

- using **stronger** magnets
- using **more turns** in the coil
- moving the **coil faster**
- moving the **magnet faster**.

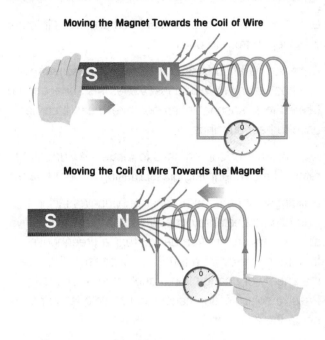

Moving the Magnet Towards the Coil of Wire

Moving the Coil of Wire Towards the Magnet

The AC Generator

In a **generator**, a coil of wire is **rotated** in a magnetic field. The coil and field should be close together.

As the coil cuts through the magnetic field, the **relative motion** causes a current to be generated in the coil.

The current **alternates**, i.e. it reverses its direction of flow, every half turn of the coil so a generator produces an **alternating current** (AC). This is different from a battery, which produces a **direct current** (DC).

The graph alongside shows an alternating current. As time passes, the line curves up into the positive area above the x-axis, and down into the negative area under the x-axis. This shows that the current alternates from a positive direction to a negative direction and back again.

The **frequency** of AC electricity is the number of **cycles** that are completed every second. For example, in the graph, it takes 4 seconds for one cycle, so the frequency is 0.25 cycles per second (1 cycle ÷ 4 seconds = 0.25Hz).

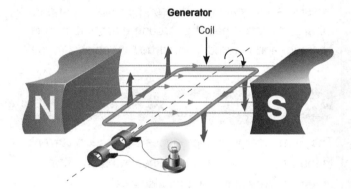

Generator

Coil

Alternating Current

Key Words   Dynamo effect • Magnetic field • Current • Alternating current • Direct current

Producing Electricity

Electricity is produced in **power stations**:

1. The fuel (energy source) is **burned** to release heat energy.
2. The heat boils water to produce **steam**.
3. The steam drives the **turbines**, which drive **generators**.
4. The generators produce **electricity**.

The electricity produced in power stations is distributed around the country by a network of power lines called the **National Grid**. It is distributed to consumers, e.g. homes, businesses, factories, offices and farms.

A significant amount of the energy produced by conventional power stations is **wasted**.

At each stage in the electricity transfer process, energy is transferred to the **surroundings** in a 'non-useful' form, usually as **heat**.

The energy transfer diagram for the process shows how much energy is wasted at each stage. The overall efficiency is only 30%.

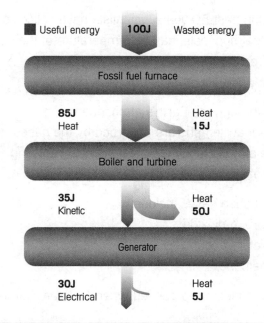

Efficiency of a Power Station

You can use the following equation to calculate the **efficiency** of a power station:

$$\text{Efficiency} = \frac{\text{Electrical energy output (J)}}{\text{Fuel energy input (J)}} \, (\times \, 100)$$

Example

A power station uses 200 000J of fuel energy to produce 80 000J of electrical energy.

What is the efficiency of the power station?

$$\text{Efficiency} = \frac{\text{Electrical energy output}}{\text{Fuel energy input}} \, (\times \, 100)$$

$$= \frac{80\,000\text{J}}{200\,000\text{J}} \, (\times \, 100) = \textbf{0.4 or 40\%}$$

Remember, answers can be left as a ratio.

P2 Global Warming

Global Warming

Many **greenhouse gases** occur naturally. Greenhouse gases in the atmosphere trap heat and warm the Earth sufficiently to support life.

Over the past 50 years, scientists have collected data that suggests that the temperature of the Earth is increasing. This is called **global warming**.

Most electromagnetic radiation from the Sun can pass through the Earth's atmosphere.
Some wavelengths are absorbed by the gases in the atmosphere. This prevents heat radiating into space.

Greenhouse gases include:
- carbon dioxide
- water vapour
- methane.

These gases are produced when fuels are burned.

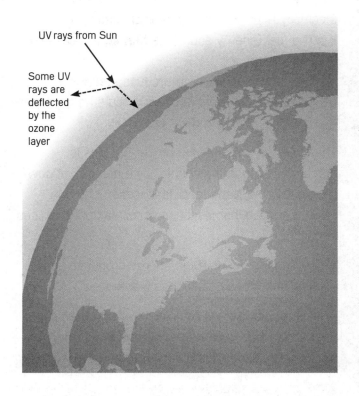

UV rays from Sun

Some UV rays are deflected by the ozone layer

Causes of Global Warming

Although many scientists agree that the average temperature of the atmosphere is increasing, they disagree about why it's happening.

Some believe that the Earth is following a natural cycle, whilst others believe that man's activity on Earth (burning fossil fuels and increased industry) is to blame.

Causes of Global Warming (Cont.)

The table below shows evidence which supports manmade global warming and evidence which refutes (disagrees with) it.

Supports	Refutes
• Humans are burning more fossil fuels. • The amount of carbon dioxide in the atmosphere is increasing. • Greenhouse gases trap heat and prevent it from escaping into space. • The average temperature of the planet is increasing.	• The temperature of the Earth changes over time (increasing and decreasing in a 40 000 year cycle). • The increase in carbon dioxide in the atmosphere is not significant enough to affect global temperatures. • Water vapour has a much more significant effect on global warming. • The surface temperatures of Mercury and Venus have increased, which isn't due to humans.

Some statements are **evidence-based**. This means that they're based upon data gathered from scientific experiments, or on data collated from previous studies. Some statements are **opinion-based**. This means that they haven't been tested scientifically.

Scientists may agree that the average temperature of the Earth has increased, but still disagree as to the cause.

More studies may be needed to determine whether global warming is due to human activity. Before data is universally accepted, it must be **repeatable** by other scientists, and **verified** as **accurate**.

HT The Greenhouse Effect

The greenhouse effect occurs because short wavelength electromagnetic radiation from the Sun is absorbed by the Earth, causing it to heat up. The Earth then radiates heat as **longer wavelength** infrared radiation. Greenhouse gases absorb some of these longer wavelength infrared waves, warming the atmosphere.

Quick Test

1. What is meant by the term 'renewable energy'?
2. What are the three factors that affect the power output of a photocell?
3. What are the four stages of electricity production in a conventional power station?
4. Name two greenhouse gases.

Power Station Fuels

This table shows the fuels that are commonly used in power stations:

Type of Fuel	Examples	Method of Releasing Energy
Fossil fuel	• Crude oil • Coal • Natural gas	Fuel burned to release heat energy.
Biomass	• Wood • Straw • Manure	Biomass fermented to generate methane.
Nuclear fuel	• Uranium	Fuel rods release heat energy.

Distributing Electricity

The electricity produced in power stations is distributed around the country by a network of power lines called the **National Grid**. The electricity has to be transmitted at very high voltage (about 40 000V) to reduce heat loss and costs.

Transformers are used to increase and decrease the voltage before and after transmission. The voltage is too high for use by consumers so **transformers** are used to reduce the voltage for safe use. A transformer that does this is called a **step-down transformer**.

(HT) As an electric current is transmitted along a wire, the wire heats up due to collisions within the material. The wire loses this heat to the environment.

If the electricity is transmitted at a higher voltage (but the power remains the same), the current in the wire is reduced. A lower current means less heating of the wires, so less energy lost from the wires as heat.

(HT) Off-Peak Electricity

There is a lower demand for electricity at night because most people are asleep.

To encourage consumers to use electricity during the night-time period, electricity companies offer an off-peak rate for 7 hours every night, which is called **Economy-7**.

The advantages and disadvantage of Economy-7 are listed in the table.

Advantages
• Less demand for electricity at night.
• Cheaper electricity for the consumer.
• Avoids wasting electrical energy.

Disadvantage
• Inconvenient to run appliances at night because of the noise they make.

HT Comparing Energy Sources

The table below lists the advantages and disadvantages of different types of fuels and renewable energy sources.

Source	Advantages	Disadvantages
Fossil fuel, e.g. coal, oil, gas	• Relatively cheap and easy to obtain. • Enough reserves for short to medium term. • Coal-, oil- and gas-fired power stations are flexible in meeting demand and have a relatively quick start-up time. • Burning gas doesn't produce SO_2.	• Burning produces CO_2 which causes global warming, and SO_2 (except burning gas) which causes acid rain. • Removing SO_2 from waste gases (to reduce global warming) adds to the cost. • Oil is often carried between continents in tankers, leading to risk of spillage and pollution. • Expensive pipelines and networks are often required to transport it to the point of use.
Biomass, e.g. wood, straw, manure	• It is renewable.	• Produces CO_2 and SO_2 which damage the environment. • Large area is needed to grow trees, which could be used for other purposes, e.g. growing food.
Nuclear fuel, e.g. uranium	• Cost and rate of fuel production is relatively low. • Can be situated in sparsely populated areas. • Nuclear power stations are flexible in meeting demand. • Doesn't produce CO_2 or SO_2 (greenhouse gases). • High stocks of nuclear fuel. • Can reduce use of fossil fuels.	• Radioactive material can stay dangerously radioactive for thousands of years and can be harmful. • Storing radioactive waste is very expensive. • Building and decommissioning nuclear power stations are costly processes. • Comparatively long start-up time. • Risk of accidental release of radioactive material. • High maintenance costs.
Renewable sources, e.g. wind, tidal, hydroelectric, solar	• Produce clean electricity. • Can be constructed in remote areas. • No fuel costs during operation. • No chemical pollution. • Often low maintenance. • Don't contribute to global warming or produce acid rain once set up.	• With the exception of hydroelectric, they produce small amounts of electricity. • Take up lots of space and are unsightly. • Unreliable (apart from hydroelectric), dependent on the weather and cannot guarantee supply on demand. • High initial capital outlay.

P2 Fuels for Power

Power

An **electric current** is the flow of electric charge from the battery (or other power supply) to the components in the circuit. The components then transfer the energy, for example, a lamp changes electrical energy into light energy.

The **rate** of the **energy transfer** determines the power of the component or device and is measured in:

- joules per second (J/s)
- **watts** (W) – 1 watt is the transfer of 1 joule of energy in 1 second.
- kilowatts (kW) – 1kW is the same as 1000W.

You can calculate the **power** of an appliance using this formula:

> **Power (W)** ═ **Current (A)** ✕ **Voltage (V)**

Example

Calculate the power of a lamp when the current flowing through it is 0.3A and the voltage across it is 3V.

Power = Current × Voltage
= 0.3A × 3V
= **0.9 watts**

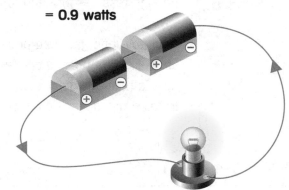

Kilowatt Hours

The power of an appliance is measured in watts (W) or kilowatts (kW). 1kW = 1000W. A **kilowatt hour** (kWh) is a measure of how much electrical energy has been used.

The number of kWh units of electricity used by an appliance depends on:

- the **power rating** (in kilowatts, kW) of the appliance
- the **time** (in hours, h) that the appliance is switched on for.

You can use the following formula to calculate the cost of using an appliance for a certain length of time:

> **Total cost (p)** ═ **Number of kilowatt hours used (kWh)** ✕ **Cost per unit (p)**

Example

If electricity costs 8p per kWh, what is the cost of using 3kWh?

Total cost = Number of kWh used × Cost per unit
= 3kWh × 8p = **24p**

(HT) Use this formula to calculate energy supplied:

> **Energy supplied (kWh)** ═ **Power (kW)** ✕ **Time (h)**

N.B. When doing these calculations the power needs to be in kilowatts, and the time needs to be in hours.

Example

A 1.5kW electric hot plate was switched on for 2 hours. How much electricity was supplied?

Energy supplied = Power × Time
= 1.5kW × 2h = **3kWh**

Quick Test

1. Name three types of fuel used in power stations.
2. Nuclear power is **not** a 'renewable source'. Why?
3. State the equation used to calculate electrical power.

Transfer • Power • Kilowatt hour

Background Radiation

Radioactive **materials** are substances that give out **nuclear radiation** all the time. Radioactivity involves a **change** in the structure of the radioactive atom and the **release** of one or more of the three types of nuclear radiation: **alpha** (α), **beta** (β) and **gamma** (γ).

Radiation that occurs naturally all around us is called **background radiation**. It only provides a very small dose, so there is no danger to our health. Some sources of background radiation include:
- radioactive substances in rocks, soil and living things
- **cosmic rays** from outer space and the Sun.

Penetration and Ionisation

Each type of radiation has a different **penetrative** power, i.e. the different radiations can pass through different thicknesses of different materials.

Alpha, beta and gamma radiations cause **ionisation** that can **damage** 'healthy' molecules in **living cells**, resulting in the death of the cell. This can also lead to **cancer**.

People who handle radioactive materials need to take safety measures such as:
- wearing protective clothing
- keeping their distance by using tongs to hold the material whenever possible
- trying to minimise their exposure time
- storing radioactive materials in clearly labelled, **shielded** containers.

Radiation can also be beneficial.

Particle	Ionising Power	Penetrating Power
Alpha	Strong	Absorbed by a few centimetres of air or thin paper.
Beta	Reasonable	Passes through air and paper. Absorbed by a few millimetres of aluminium.
Gamma	Weak	Very penetrating. Needs many centimetres of lead or metres of concrete to stop it.

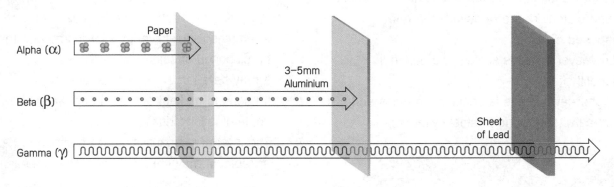

You can identify whether radiation is alpha, beta or gamma by finding out what material it can penetrate.

During ionisation, a particle gains or loses electrons, leaving the atom charged. A gain in electrons gives a negative ion and if the atom loses electrons it becomes a positive ion.

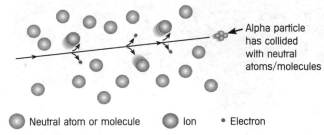

Alpha particle has collided with neutral atoms/molecules

Neutral atom or molecule   Ion   • Electron

P2 Nuclear Radiations

Use of Alpha Radiation

Most **smoke detectors** contain Americium-241, which emits alpha **radiation**. The emitted alpha particles **ionise** air particles and the **ions** formed are **attracted** to the oppositely charged **electrodes**. This produces a **current** in the circuit.

When smoke enters the space between the two electrodes, less ionisation takes place as the alpha particles are absorbed by the smoke particles. A smaller current then flows, which triggers an alarm.

Uses of Beta Radiation

A **tracer** is a small amount of a **radioactive substance** that is put into a system so that its progress through the system can be followed using a radiation detector.

A beta emitter tracer can be used to observe how elements such as nitrogen and phosphorus move through a plant, from root to leaf.

Beta radiation is used in a **paper thickness gauge**. When beta radiation passes through the paper, some of it is absorbed. If the paper thickness is too great, more beta radiation is absorbed and less passes through to the detector. This indicates that the thickness of the paper needs to be reduced.

Uses of Gamma Radiation

Gamma radiation can be used to **treat cancer** because it destroys cancerous cells. But care must be taken not to destroy the healthy cells. It can also be used to **sterilise medical equipment** because it can destroy microorganisms like bacteria.

Non-destructive **tests** can be carried out on welds using gamma radiation, by placing a gamma source on one side of the material. Any cracks or defects are then identified using a detector (e.g. photographic film) on the other side.

Dealing with Radioactive Waste

Spent fuel is taken to be **reprocessed** – the unused fuel and plutonium are removed. The rest is **disposed** of:

- Low-level waste is sealed and buried in landfill sites.
- Higher-level waste is enclosed in glass and stored underground in steel cylinders.

(HT) There are four main **problems** to bear in mind when dealing with radioactive waste:

- It remains radioactive for a long time and must be disposed of safely.
- It may be a target for terrorist activity.
- It needs to be kept out of ground water to avoid contaminating drinking supplies.
- The level of radioactivity that's deemed to be acceptable may change over time, so measures may need to be modified.

Quick Test

1. Which type of radiation is the most penetrating?
2. Give two uses of gamma radiation.
3. How is high-level radioactive waste stored?

Ion • Current • Tracer

The Universe

The Universe is made up of:

- **planets**, **comets** and **meteors**
- **stars**, e.g. our Sun – they can be clearly seen even though they are far away because they are very hot and give out light
- **galaxies** – large groups of stars
- **black holes** – dense, dying stars with a strong gravitational field.

(HT) Black holes can be found throughout the Universe and in every galaxy. They have a **very large mass** concentrated into a **very small space**. This means that their **gravity** is very **large**; this is why nothing can escape from black holes – not even light.

Orbits in the Solar System

The Sun is in the centre of our Solar System. The eight planets (including Earth) and comets move around the Sun in slightly squashed circles (ellipses) called **orbits**.

Satellites orbit planets. The moon is a satellite that is in orbit around the Earth.

Planets, comets and satellites are kept in their orbits by the **gravitational force** of the larger object they are orbiting.

(HT) The planets, comets and satellites travel in circular (or near circular) paths around a larger object. They stay in their orbits because the larger object exerts an **inward pull force** on them.

This inward pull force is provided by **gravity** and is called the **centripetal force**, e.g. the Earth orbits the Sun because of the gravitational pull force of the Sun.

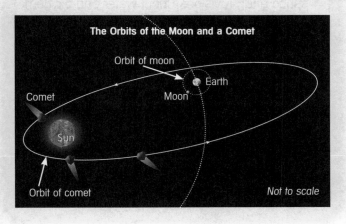

The Orbits of the Moon and a Comet

Orbit of moon
Earth
Comet
Moon
Sun
Orbit of comet
Not to scale

The Sun and the Planets in the Solar System

Sun
Mercury
Venus
Earth
Mars
Jupiter
Saturn
Uranus
Neptune
Pluto
Not to scale

N.B. Pluto has been known as a dwarf planet since September 2006.

P2 Exploring Our Solar System

Manned Space Travel

Space is a very dangerous place. There are many **difficulties** which face a **manned** space mission to the planets.

Here are some problems with manned space missions:

- The planets are very, very far away so it can take months or years to reach them.
- The fuel required takes up most of the spacecraft.

- Room must be found to store enough food, water and oxygen for the whole journey.
- A stable artificial atmosphere must be maintained in the spacecraft.
- The temperature in space is freezing, so keeping warm is vitally important.
- Outside of the Earth's magnetic field, humans need shielding from cosmic rays.
- The low **gravity** affects people's health.
- Radio signals take a very long time to reach the Earth!

Unmanned Space Travel

A far more safe and realistic option is to explore our Solar System using **unmanned** spacecraft.

As well as being able to withstand conditions that are lethal to humans, these probes don't require food, water or oxygen.

Once they arrive on a planet, probes can be used to send back information about the planet's:

- temperature
- magnetic field
- radiation levels
- gravity
- atmosphere
- surrounding landscape.

Samples from nearby (the moon) can be brought back to Earth for analysis.

(HT) Once a probe arrives on a planet, it can send information to Earth through radio waves which travel at the speed of light. The distance light travels in a year is called a **light year**. This measurement is used when talking about **very large distances**.

This table lists the advantages and disadvantages of using unmanned spacecraft:

Advantages
• Costs are lower as there is no need to provide space and provisions (food, water and oxygen) for human passengers.
• With no humans aboard, safety is no longer a consideration.

Disadvantages
• Reliability has to be high as there will be no one to fix any breakdowns.
• Instruments must require zero maintenance.

Asteroids

Asteroids are rocks left over from the formation of the Solar System. They normally **orbit** the Sun in a **belt** between Mars and Jupiter but occasionally they get knocked off course and head towards Earth.

When an asteroid **collides** with Earth there can be several devastating **consequences**:

- An impact would form a crater, which could trigger the ejection of hot rocks.
- The heat may cause widespread fires.
- Sunlight could be blocked out by the dust from an explosion (so plants wouldn't be able to photosynthesise).
- It could trigger a climate change.
- Whole species could become extinct.

There is evidence to suggest that asteroids have collided with Earth many times in the past:

- Craters can be found all over the planet.
- There are layers of unusual elements found in rocks.
- There are sudden changes in the number of fossils found in adjacent rock layers, which could be due to the sudden death of many animals.

(HT) When asteroids in the belt of asteroids between Jupiter and Mars bump into each other they can join up or shatter. They can't combine to form a new planet because the larger mass formed feels a greater pull from Jupiter's strong gravitational field and is attracted to it and breaks up.

Comets

A **comet** is a small body with a core of frozen gas (ice) and dust. The characteristic tail is a trail of debris. Comets come from the objects that orbit the Sun. Comets have **highly elliptical orbits** around the Sun. The **speed** of the comet **increases** as it approaches the Sun.

(HT) The comet's speed increases as a result of the increase in the strength of **gravity** as it approaches the star (Sun). It can also be affected by the gravity of planets.

Near Earth Objects (NEOs)

A **Near Earth Object** is an asteroid or comet that is on a possible collision course with Earth.

Telescopes are used to observe these objects in an attempt to determine their **trajectories** (probable paths).

(HT) Large NEOs may pose a threat to the human race, but there are actions we can take to reduce the threat:

- Survey the skies with telescopes to identify likely NEOs as early as possible.
- Monitor the object's progress with satellites.
- Deflect the object with an explosion if a collision is likely (as long as it isn't too close to Earth).

The Moon

The moon may be the remains of a planet which collided with the Earth billions of years ago. A collision between two planets could result in an Earth–moon system in this way:

- The planets collide.

- The iron cores of each planet merge to form the core of the Earth.
- Less dense material becomes the moon and begins to orbit the Earth.

P2 The Big Bang

Big Bang Theory

The **Big Bang theory** can be used to explain how the Universe arrived at its present state. The theory states:
- the Universe started **billions of years ago** in one place with a huge explosion, i.e. a **big bang**
- the Universe is **expanding**.

When we look at the stars we can observe that:
- nearly all the galaxies are moving away from us
- distant galaxies are moving away more quickly
- microwave radiation is received from all parts of the Universe.

(HT) **Red shift** is the shifting of the wavelengths of light towards the red end of the spectrum. It can be observed in the light we receive from galaxies. The further away a galaxy is, the greater the red shift. This means that galaxies further away from us are travelling faster than those closer to us.

Measuring red shift provides **evidence** for the expansion of the Universe. By tracking the movement of the galaxies, we can **estimate** the age and starting point of the Universe.

The Life of a Star

(HT) A **proto-star** is formed when interstellar gas clouds collapse under gravitational attraction. Then thermonuclear fusion reactions take place, releasing massive amounts of energy and increasing the star's temperature. During this time, the star experiences a long period of normal life (**main sequence**). But, eventually, the supply of hydrogen runs out, causing the end of the star. The type of end depends largely on the **mass** of the star.

Stars start as huge clouds of gas. They have a **finite** (limited) life, depending on the star's supply of hydrogen. Stars are different sizes. Their size determines how they change during the end stages of their life.

End stages of a **heavy-weight star**:
1. Star swells up to form a **red supergiant**.
2. The red supergiant rapidly shrinks and explodes, releasing massive amounts of energy, dust and gas into space. This is a **supernova**.
3. The next stage depends on the size of the star:
   - The remnants of stars up to ten times the mass of our Sun form a **neutron star**, which is made of very dense matter.
   - Stars greater than ten times the mass of our Sun leave behind **black holes**. Black holes can only be observed indirectly through their effects on their surroundings – light cannot escape from a black hole because its gravitational pull is too big.

End stages of a **medium-weight star** (like our Sun):
1. Star swells up to form a red giant.
2. The core of the red giant contracts (shrinks) to be surrounded by outer shells of gas (**planetary nebula**).
3. The core cools and contracts to become a white dwarf, with a density thousands of times greater than any matter on Earth.

End Stages of a Heavy-Weight Star

Star
↓
Red supergiant
↓
Supernova
↓
Neutron star   Black hole

End Stages of a Medium-Weight Star

Star
↓
Red giant
↓
Planetary nebula
↓
White dwarf

Key Words   Big Bang Theory • Red Shift • Thermonuclear fusion • Red giant • White dwarf

Models of the Universe

People haven't always believed that the Sun is the centre of our solar system, or that there is anything beyond the stars. A number of models of the Universe were put forward before the model accepted today.

The Ptolemaic Model of the Universe

The **Ptolemaic model** stated that the Earth was the centre of the Universe (the **geocentric model**) and that the Earth was surrounded by crystal spheres which held the other planets and the stars.

The Copernican Model of the Universe

The **Copernican model** was proposed in the 16th century by the astronomer **Copernicus**.
Many of its ideas were the same as the Ptolemaic model:

* The planets sat on spheres, a fixed distance from the Sun.
* The stars were fixed on the outermost sphere and didn't move.

But, the Copernican model differed from the Ptolemaic model in the following ways.
It stated that:

* the Sun is the centre of the Universe
* the Earth rotated once every 24 hours
* the Earth takes one year to revolve around the Sun.

Galileo

Later in the 16th century, **Galileo** used telescopes to observe the surface of the moon. He discovered that it wasn't a perfect sphere (all heavenly bodies were thought to be perfect spheres at that time). He also discovered four moons orbiting Jupiter.

He later discovered that Venus has phases like the moon, which meant that Venus couldn't be attached to a crystal sphere, but that it orbited the Sun, like the Earth.

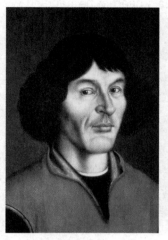
Nicolaus Copernicus

Galileo Galilei

(HT) The theories of Copernicus and Galileo were not widely accepted. Their ideas were in direct opposition to the Catholic Church's belief that the Earth was the centre of the Universe.

It took many years before Galileo's theory of the nature of the Universe was accepted.

Advances in technology, and the ability to build more powerful telescopes led to observations that supported the **heliocentric theory** (that the Sun was the centre of the Solar System).

Quick Test

1. What is an asteroid?
2. What is a comet?
3. What will a medium weight star, like our Sun, eventually become?

1. David works for a nuclear power station. He has to work with radioactive materials on a daily basis.

    a) Radioactive materials need to be handled with care. Describe the safety precautions David must take. **[3]**

    b) Radiation occurs naturally all around us, but it only provides a small dose so it is harmless. Describe two sources of background radiation. **[2]**

    c) Give one use for each type of radiation. **[3]**

        i) Alpha: ....   ii) Beta: ....   iii) Gamma: ....

2. a) How can you generate an electric current in a wire? **[1]**

    b) Describe three ways to increase the current generated by the dynamo effect. **[3]**

3. a) A coal-fired power station provides 50 000J of electrical energy for every 150 000J of coal it burns. Calculate the efficiency of the power station. **[2]**

    b) Describe the four stages of power generation in the coal-fired power station. **[2]**

4 Suggest two pieces of evidence that show that asteroids collided with the Earth in the past. **[2]**

5 a) A 1200W hairdryer is used for 15 minutes. How many kilowatt hours of electricity does it use? **[2]**

b) An oven uses 3kWh of energy during a 2 hour period. What is its power rating? **[2]**

6 Describe the similarities and differences between the Ptolemaic and Copernican models of the Universe. **[6]**

✐ *The quality of your written communication will be assessed in your answer to this question.*

HT 7 Most asteroids are found between Mars and Jupiter. Explain why these rocks do not join together to form new planets. **[2]**

Answers

B1 Understanding Organisms

Quick Test Answers

Page 7
1. Being overweight, stress, high alcohol intake, smoking, exercise, diet, particularly salt.
2. Mass (kg) ÷ height (m)^2
3. Arthritis, heart disease, type II diabetes, breast cancer.
4. Overpopulation, limited investment in agricultural techniques.

Page 11
1. Bacteria, fungi, viruses.
2. Harmless dead or weakened pathogen is given in an injection, the body makes antibodies which remain in the blood to fight future infection.
3. Mosquito nets, insecticides, insect repellents.

Page 14
1. **Any one from:** Knee jerk; Pupil reflex; Dropping a hot plate
2. Binocular   **3.** Convex lens

Page 16
1. **Any two from:** Impaired judgement; Poor balance; Blurred vision; Slurred speech; Drowsiness; Vasodilation.
2. Red because the smoke is acidic.
3. Tar and particulates.

Page 18
1. Maintaining a constant internal environment.
2. Failure of the pancreas to produce insulin.
3. In the blood.
4. Slower

Page 21
1. Plant hormones   **2.** XX   **3.** Faulty genes

Answers to Exam Practice Questions
1. Lack of balance / muscle control; Blurred vision; Lack of inhibitions; Slurred speech; Drowsiness; Poor judgement; Vasodilation **[Any four for 4]**
2. a) Using a (clinical) thermometer in mouth/under armpit/in ear/in anus; Using an electronic probe in mouth/under armpit/in ear/in anus. **[Any one for 1]**
   b) Yes he could be ill; Normal body temperature is 37°C.
   c) Mucus is made **should be ticked d)** Virus
3. a) XX   **b)** Alleles
4. a) Rates of smoking (males and females) have decreased; Males have a higher percentage of smoking in all years.
   b) Male cancer rates have fallen steadily; Female cancer rates have increased.
5. a) They become addicted to / dependent on nicotine.
   b) BMI = 34.6
      Yes, he is obese because his BMI is over 30.
   c) Yes, because he is obese.
   d) i) The one with LJ3; The sample size was larger.
      ii) Both drugs help people to lose weight; ULose is more effective than LJ3; But even taking a placebo resulted in some weight loss. **[Any two for 2]**
      iii) These were the control group; To prevent bias in reporting results.
   e) **Any two from:** Drug fits / blocks the receptor site / molecule; Stops the neurotransmitter getting into receptor site / molecule; Receptor is on the membrane of next neurone.
6. No, eggs are protein; Proteins are not stored in the body.

B2 Understanding Our Environment

Quick Test Answers

Page 27
1. A position or stage that an organism occupies in a food chain.
2. Crustacean, Insect, Arachnid, Myriapod
3. Heat, respiration, excretion, egestion.
4. They don't fit easily into any group.

Page 29
1. Nitrogen, carbon.
2. 78%
3. Convert ammonia to nitrates.

Page 31
1. a) Parasites
   b) **Any suitable example, e.g.** the oxpecker bird and buffalo.
2. Intraspecific.

Page 35
1. Charles Darwin
2. If they are unable to compete, due to climate change, destruction of habitat, hunting, pollution, competition.
3. **Any suitable example, e.g.** The peppered moth – dark and pale forms; Bacteria becoming resistant to antibiotics; Rats resistant to poisons.
4. They didn't agree with the Church or the Bible.

Page 37
1. Acid rain
2. Their presence or absence helps to indicate levels of pollution.
3. The amount of greenhouse gases given off in a given time per person or by an action or event.

Page 39
1. a) An animal or plant in danger of becoming extinct as numbers are so low.
   b) Protect habitats, legal protection, education programmes, captive breeding programmes, seed banks, creating artificial breeding programmes.
2. When alive – tourism; When dead – food, oil, cosmetics.
3. Sets quotas.

Answers to Exam Practice Questions
1. a) Quotas mean enough can be left to reproduce and so maintain the species.
   b) **Any two from:** Other countries may keep fishing; People may fish illegally; Global warming; Habitat destruction; Pollution; Disease; Lack of food.
2. a) Thick fur – for insulation / to keep warm / to stop heat loss; Layer of fat – for insulation; Small ears – reduce heat loss; Large feet – spread load on snow / to stop them sinking; White fur – camouflage for hunting; Fur on paws – for insulation / grip; Large body size – small SA to V / mass ratio **[Any two for 4]**
   b) **This is a model answer, which demonstrates QWC and therefore would score the full 6 marks:** The polar bear has adapted to live in a habitat of polar ice caps, so if the habitat changes, the polar bear may not be able to survive. Polar bear numbers would decline. They would no longer be camouflaged due to there being no snow or ice. Their thick coat and blubber / fat may cause them to overheat in the warmer temperatures, and the change to their habitat may lead to a lack of breeding ground.
3. a) C; No mechanisms for movement.
   b) Monera/Prokaryotes **[1]** It is single-celled; It has no nucleus. **[Any one for 1]**
   c) Animals; It uses legs (muscles) to move.
4. a) Canis lupus
   b) Zebra and donkey; Zebra and horse; Donkey and horse **[Any one for 1]** They belong to the same genus **[1]**
5. Shape reduces water loss; Thick waxy cuticle reduces water loss; Storing water in spongy layer inside stem; Green stem allows photosynthesis without leaves; Long roots to reach water; Spines to protect from animals. **[Any four for 4]**
6. a) There isn't enough energy to pass on.
   b) 120 ÷ 2200 = 5.5% **[1 for calculation, 1 for correct answer]**

Answers

Chemistry

Fundamental Chemical Concepts

Quick Test Answers
Page 45
1. Electrons
2. In the nucleus.
3. A charged atom or group of atoms that has lost or gained electrons.
4. The different types of atom in a compound; The number of each type of atom; Where the bonds are in the compound.

C1 Carbon Chemistry

Quick Test Answers
Page 47
1. A resource that is being used up faster than it can be replaced.
2. Hydrogen and carbon.
3. Liquefied petroleum gas (LPG).
4. a) Breaking down a large hydrocarbon into smaller alkanes and alkenes. b) To increase the amount of the petrol fraction and to make alkenes that can be used for making polymers.

Page 49
1. Incomplete combustion (of a hydrocarbon).
2. Blue.
3. Oxygen.
4. $CH_4 + 2O_2 \rightarrow CO_2 + 2H_2O$
5. $2CH_4 + 3O_2 \rightarrow 2CO + 4H_2O$ or $CH_4 + O_2 \rightarrow C + 2H_2O$

Page 51
1. Nitrogen and oxygen.
2. Respiration and combustion.
3. Ammonia and carbon dioxide.
4. Photochemical smog and acid rain.

Page 55
1. A long-chain molecule made of small repeating units called monomers.
2. Poly(ethene).
3. **Any two from:** It is lightweight; It is waterproof; It is tough; It can easily be coloured.

Page 57
1. **Any one from:** Meat; Eggs; Fish.
2. a) Sodium hydrogencarbonate b) Thermal decomposition c) sodium hydrogencarbonate $\xrightarrow{heat}$ carbon dioxide + water + sodium carbonate d) carbon dioxide gas.
3. When protein molecules change shape as they are cooked.

Page 61
1. **Any suitable answer, e.g.** Lavender; Musk; Rose.
2. So that it does not wash off your skin easily.
3. A type of mixture.

4. Pigment, binding medium and a solvent.
5. To protect and decorate.
6. The solvent evaporates and the oil binding medium oxidises in the air.

Answers to Exam Practice Questions
1. a) The fractions can be separated and collected because hydrocarbons [1] boil at different temperatures [1].
   b) Breaking up large hydrocarbon molecules into small hydrocarbon molecules [1]; To match supply and demand; To make more petrol; To make ethene **[Any one for 1]**.
   c) Small molecules have fewer forces of attraction between molecules than large molecules [1]; Less energy is needed to separate them [1].
2. a) Nitrogen
   b) 21%
   c) **Any suitable answer e.g.** carbon dioxide.
3. a) All the fuel is burned in a blue flame (complete combustion); only some of the fuel's energy is released in a yellow flame (incomplete combustion).
   b) methane + oxygen $\rightarrow$ carbon dioxide + water
4. a) A small molecule that will join up to make a polymer.
   b) Catalyst; High pressure.
5. The material has pores [1] that are too small to allow water droplets through (from the outside) [1], but are big enough to allow water vapour through (from the inside) [1].
6. **This is a model answer, which demonstrates QWC and would therefore score the full 6 marks:** The emulsifier is made of a hydrophilic head and a hydrophobic tail. The hydrophilic head forms intermolecular forces of attraction with water molecules. The hydrophobic head forms intermolecular forces of attraction with the oil molecules. This allows the oil and water to remain mixed.

Answers

C2 Chemical Resources

Quick Test Answers

Page 66
1. Crust and top part of mantle.
2. They are less dense than the mantle.
3. Earthquakes and volcanoes.
4. Magma or lava that has solidified.
5. The slower the rock cools, the larger the crystals, or reverse argument.
6. Runny and has 'safe' eruptions.

Page 70
1. As ores.
2. **Any suitable answer, e.g.** Limestone; Marble; Granite.
3. Clay and limestone are heated together.
4. It is cheaper and can reduce the use of limited natural resources.
5. A mixture of a metal with another element.
6. It is transparent.
7. Water and oxygen (in the air).

Page 74
1. Nitrogen and hydrogen.
2. 450°C, 200 atmospheres and an iron catalyst.
3. A reaction that can go forwards or backwards under the same conditions.
4. A chemical with a pH of less than 7.
5. A chemical with a pH above 7, which can dissolve in water (a soluble base).
6. acid + metal carbonate → salt + water + carbon dioxide

Page 76
1. A chemical that gives plants essential chemicals needed for growth.
2. Nitrogen, potassium and phosphorus.
3. Ammonia and sulfuric acid.
4. They use it to make protein.

Page 77
1. Sodium hydroxide, hydrogen and chlorine.
2. By reacting chlorine and sodium hydroxide together.

3. **Any suitable answer, e.g.** To sterilise water; To make household bleach; To make plastics (e.g. PVC); To make solvents.

Answers to Exam Practice Questions

1. The crust and the outer part of the mantle.
2. Slate – Natural
   Steel – Manufactured
   Cement – Manufactured
   Marble – Natural
   Brick – Manufactured
   [All correct for 3 marks, 4 correct for 2 marks, 2 or 3 correct for 1 mark]
3. a) It is heated with carbon.
   b) i) Copper(II) sulfate.
      ii) Pure copper.
      iii) Impure copper.
4. Air / oxygen; Water.
5. It saves resources **[1]** and reduces disposal problems **[1]**.
6. a) To increase the yield of their crop.
   b) Replaces essential elements used by the previous crop; Provides extra essential elements; More nitrogen gets into the plant protein, increasing its strength. **[Any two for 2]**
7. a) Air/oxygen; Water
   b) 72%
   c) 450°C
   d) 400 atmospheres
   e) Yield decreases
8. a) Ammonia solution; Ammonia hydroxide; Ammonia. **[Any one for 1]**
   b) $NH_3 + HNO_3$ → NH_4NO_3 **[1 mark for each correct formula]**
9. Where a continental plate and an oceanic plate collide. The more dense oceanic plate is pushed under **[1]** the continental plate down into the mantle where it melts **[1]**. The result is a mountain range and possibly volcanoes **[1]**.

Physics

P1 Energy for the Home

Quick Test Answers

Page 82
1. Temperature °C, energy in joules
2. The yellow one.

Page 85
1. Double glazing
2. Light and sound.

Page 87
1. Number of complete waves passing a point each second.
2. **Any two from:** Ultraviolet; X-rays; Gamma rays
3. Gap size equals wavelength of wave.

Page 91
1. **Any two from:** Satellite communications; Mobile phones; Radar.
2. Water and fat.
3. It is totally internally reflected.

Page 94
1. S-Waves
2. True

Answers to Exam Practice Questions

1. a) The ice cream is melting.
   b) The energy needed to raise the temperature of 1kg of material by 1°C.
   c) Energy transferred = Mass (kg) × specific heat capacity (J/kgC) × temperature change. 0.063kg × (1.67×10^3) × 5 = 526J **[1 for calculation, 1 for correct answer]**
2. Efficiency = $\frac{20}{1000}$ = 0.2 or 20% **[1 for calculation, 1 for correct answer]**
3. Microwaves are absorbed **[1]** by the water/fat molecules **[1]** in the outside layers of the food. The heat energy is then transferred **[1]** throughout the rest of the food by conduction and convection **[1]**.
4. **A** Crest **B** Trough **C** Amplitude **D** Wavelength
5. 890 000 × 337 = 299 930 000 m/s or 300 000 000 m/s **[1 for calculation, 1 for correct answer]**
6. a) P-waves; S-waves b) S-waves
7. 6 mins × 20 = 120 mins = 2 hours **[1 for calculation, 1 for correct answer]**
8. a) 20 years; 30 years; 1.5 years
   b) **Any suitable suggestion with explanation,** e.g. Draft excluders because they have the lowest cost/shortest payback time; Double glazing because it has the biggest annual saving.
   c) Foil reflects **[1]** heat energy (infrared) **[1]** back into room/less heat loss **[1]** so he can turn radiators down **[1]**.

P2 Living for the Future (Energy Resources)

Quick Test Answers

Page 103

1. An energy resource that will not run out.
2. Surface area, light intensity and distance from the light source.
3. Burn fuel; Heat water to produce steam; Turn turbine; Turn generator.
4. **Any two from:** Carbon dioxide; Water vapour; Methane.

Page 106

1. Fossil fuels; Biomass; Nuclear.
2. The uranium fuel will run out.
3. Power = Current × Voltage

Page 108

1. Gamma
2. **Any two from:** To treat cancer; To sterilise medical equipment; In non-destructive testing; Tracers
3. Encased in glass, then placed in steel cylinders underground.

Page 113

1. Rock left over from the formation of the Universe.
2. A small body of frozen ice and dust.
3. A white dwarf.

Answers to Exam Practice Questions

1. **a)** He must wear protective clothing; He must use tongs and keep his distance from the radioactive materials; He needs to ensure only a short exposure time; All radioactive materials must be stored in shielded and labelled containers. **[Any three for 3]**
   b) Cosmic rays (from the sun and outer space); Radioactive substances in rocks, soil and living things
   c) i) Smoke alarms.
   ii) Tracer; Thickness gauge. **[Any one for 1]**
   iii) Tracer; Treat cancer; Sterilise medical equipment. **[Any one for 1]**

2. **a)** Move it inside of a magnetic field.
   b) Use stronger magnets; Use more turns in the coil; Move the coil faster.

3. **a)** Efficiency $= \frac{50\,000}{150\,000} = 0.33$ or 33% **[1 for calculation, 1 for correct answer]**
   b) Burn fuel, heat water to produce steam, steam turns turbine, turbine turns generator. **[All correct for 2]**

4. Craters; Sudden changes in fossil record; Unusual elements. **[Any two for 2]**

5. **a)** kWh = 1.2 × 0.25 = 0.3kWh **[1 for calculation, 1 for correct answer]**
   b) Power $= \frac{Energy}{Time} = \frac{3kWh}{2\,hours} = 1.5$kW or 1500W **[1 for calculation, 1 for correct answer]**

6. **This is a model answer, which demonstrates QWC and therefore would score the full 6 marks:** The Ptolemaic and Copernican models are similar in that they both proposed that the planets sat on glass spheres a fixed distance from the Sun, and that the stars were in fixed positions on the outermost sphere. The two models are different in that the Copernican model stated that the Sun was at the centre of the Universe, the Earth rotates once every 24 hours and the Earth takes one year to revolve around the Sun. In contrast, the Ptolemaic model stated that the Earth was the centre of the Universe.

7. Jupiter's huge gravity **[1]** pulls rocks apart so they don't combine **[1]**.

Glossary of Key Words

Acid – a compound that has a pH value lower than 7.

Adaptation – the gradual change of a particular organism over generations to become better suited to its environment.

Addiction – being abnormally dependent on something; habit forming.

Additives – chemicals added to food so that they look, taste or smell better or increase their shelf-life.

Aerobic respiration – respiration using oxygen, which releases energy and produces carbon dioxide and water.

Alcohol – waste product made by yeast, following anaerobic respiration.

Alkali – a compound that has a pH value higher than 7 and can dissolve in water.

Alkane – a saturated (i.e. only single bonds) hydrocarbon.

Alkene – an unsaturated (i.e. at least one C=C) hydrocarbon.

Allele – one of two alternative forms of a particular gene.

Alloy – a mixture of two or more metals, or of a metal and a non-metal.

Alternating current (AC) – an electric current that changes direction of flow repeatedly.

Amino acids – building blocks of proteins.

Amplitude – the maximum disturbance of a wave from a central position.

Analogue – signal that varies continuously in amplitude/ frequency.

Antibiotics – medication used to kill bacterial pathogens inside the body.

Antibody – produced by white blood cells to destroy disease-causing microorganisms.

Artery – large blood vessel with narrow lumen and thick elastic walls (carries blood away from the lungs).

Arthropod – an invertebrate animal with an exoskeleton and segmented body and jointed legs.

Atmosphere – the envelope of gas around the Earth.

Atom – the smallest part of an element that can enter into chemical reactions.

Auxin – a plant hormone that affects growth and development.

Bacteria – microscopic, single-celled organism with no nucleus.

Base – a compound that has a pH greater than 7 and that will neutralise an acid.

Big Bang Theory – theory of how the Universe started.

Binary – digital signals.

Binocular – binocular vision uses two eyes to judge distances.

Biomass – the mass of matter in a living organism.

Black hole – formed at the end of a star's life, has a very dense core which light cannot escape from.

Blood pressure – the pressure of the blood in arteries and veins.

Captivity – being held or confined to a certain space, e.g. cage.

Carbohydrates – foods that provide energy.

Carcinogens – cancer-causing chemicals.

Cardiovascular efficiency – a measure of how well your heart copes with cardiovascular exercise.

Catalyst – a substance that is used to speed up a chemical reaction without being chemically altered itself.

Cement – a substance that sticks two other materials together; made by heating clay and limestone.

Characteristics – distinguishing features.

Cholesterol – a type of fat that builds up in the arteries.

Chromosome – a coil of DNA made up of genes, found in the nucleus of plants/animal cells.

Combustion – burning.

Competition – rivalry/struggle amongst organisms for food, space, mates, etc.

Complete combustion – burning in lots of oxygen.

Composite – a material made from two or more substances that can easily be seen, e.g. in plywood you can easily see the layers of the different wood.

Compound – a substance consisting of two or more elements chemically bonded.

Concrete – a mixture of sand, gravel, water and cement.

Conduction – transfer of thermal or electrical energy.

Conductor – material that transfers thermal or electrical energy.

Construction – building.

Consumer – an organism that eats other organisms.

Convection – transfer of heat energy without the movement of the substance.

Core – the centre of the Earth.

Corrosion – a reaction between metal and oxygen that turns it into a compound.

Covalent bond – a bond between two atoms in which one or more pairs of electrons are shared.

Cracking – breaking down (decomposition of) long chain hydrocarbons into smaller, more useful, short chain hydrocarbons.

Critical angle – the largest incident angle at which refraction can occur.

Crust – the outer layer of the Earth.

Current – the rate of flow of an electrical charge; measured in amperes (A).

Data – information collected from an experiment/investigation.

Decay – rotting, breaking down.

Decomposers – organisms that break down dead plants or animals into simpler substances.

Decomposition – a chemical reaction where a compound breaks down into simpler substances.

Deficiency – a lack of a substance.

Deforestation – destruction of forests by cutting down trees.

Degrees Celsius (°C) – unit of temperature.

Depressants – drugs that slow the way the body works, e.g. alcohol.

Diabetes – a disease caused by the failure to control blood sugar levels due to the inability of the pancreas to secrete insulin.

Diffraction – the spreading out of a wave as a result of passing an obstacle through a gap.

Digital – signal that uses only 1s and 0s.

Direct current (DC) – an electric current that only flows in one direction.

Dynamo effect – generating electricity by moving a coil of wire near a magnet.

Ecosystem – refers to a physical environment – the conditions there and the organisms that live there.

Efficiency – useful output energy expressed as a percentage of total input energy.

Egestion – the removal of undigested food and waste from an animal's body.

Electrode – the conducting rod or plate (usually metal or graphite) that allows electric current to enter and leave an electrolysis cell.

Electrolysis – the breaking down of a liquid or dissolved ionic substance using electricity.

Electrolyte – an aqueous or molten substance that contains free-moving ions and is therefore able to conduct electricity.

Electromagnetic – energy transmitted as waves.

Electromagnetic waves – includes radio waves, visible light and gamma, all of which can travel through a vacuum at the speed of light.

Electron – a negatively charged subatomic particle that orbits the nucleus of an atom.

Element – a substance that consists of only one type of atom.

Emphysema – chronic irreversible lung disease, caused by smoking.

Emulsifiers – a chemical that can be used to make sure that oil and water remain mixed.

Emulsion – a mixture of oil (fat) and water.

Endangered – organisms whose numbers are so low they are in danger of becoming extinct.

Energy – ability to do work; measured in joules.

Enzyme – a protein molecule and biological catalyst found in living organisms that helps chemical reactions to take place.

Ester – a family of chemicals that often smell nice.

Eutrophication – the excessive growth and decay of aquatic plants, e.g. algae, due to increased levels of nutrients in the water (often caused by fertilisers or untreated sewage), which results in oxygen levels dropping so that fish and other animal populations eventually die out.

Evaporation – a physical change where a liquid becomes a gas using the energy from other particles in that substance.

Evolve – to develop and change naturally over a period of time.

Extinct – an organism that no longer exists.

Fats – a wide group of compounds that provide the body with energy and insulation, e.g. butter, oil.

Fertiliser – a chemical that helps plants grow and increases the yield of crops.

Fossil fuel – coal, oil or natural gas.

Fractional distillation – a method of separating a mixture of liquids each with a different boiling point.

Frequency – the number of waves produced (or that pass a particular point) in one second.

Fungi – single-celled microscopic organisms.

Gene – a small section of DNA, in a chromosome, that determines a particular characteristic on its own or in combination with other genes.

Global warming – increase in average temperature on Earth due to rise in CO_2 in the atmosphere.

Gore-Tex® – a brand name of a breathable layered fabric which includes a layer of Teflon™ polymer.

Gravitational force – a force of attraction between masses.

Gravity (gravitational force) – a force of attraction between masses.

Greenhouse effect – the process by which the Earth is kept warm by the atmosphere reflecting heat back down towards the Earth, preventing it from escaping into space.

Haber process – an industrial process where nitrogen and hydrogen are used to make ammonia.

Homeostasis – the maintenance of constant internal conditions in the body.

Hormone – a chemical messenger that travels around the body in the blood to affect target organs.

Host – an organism that another organism lives off.

Hydrocarbon – a chemical containing only hydrogen and carbon.

Hydrophilic – water loving.

Hydrophobic – water hating.

Hypothesis – a scientific explanation that will be tested through experiments.

Immunisation – giving an injection to provide immunity from a disease.

Glossary of Key Words

Incomplete combustion – burning in a limited supply of oxygen.

Indicator – a chemical that changes colour to show changes in pH.

Indicator species – a species that acts as an indicator of pollution.

Inert – does not undergo chemical reactions easily.

Inherit – to 'receive' genes or characteristics from a parent.

Insoluble – a substance that is unable to dissolve in a solvent.

Insulator – a substance that doesn't transfer thermal or electrical energy.

Insulin – a hormone, produced by the pancreas, which controls blood glucose concentrations.

Interference – when a signal is corrupted, e.g. hissing on the radio.

Invertebrate – an animal with no backbone.

Ion – a charged particle formed when an atom gains or loses an electron.

Ionic bond – the bond formed when electrons are transferred between a metal and a non-metal atom, creating charged ions that are then held together by forces of attraction.

Ionising – radiation that turns atoms into ions.

Joule (J) – unit of energy.

Kilowatt hour – a measure of how much electrical energy has been used.

Kinetic energy (KE) – the energy possessed by a body because of its movement.

Kwashiorkor – an illness caused by protein deficiency due to lack of food.

Laser – perfectly coherent light source.

Lava – molten rock on the surface of the Earth.

Lithosphere – the crust and top part of the mantle of the Earth.

Longitudinal wave – a wave where the particles vibrate in the direction of energy transfer.

Magma – molten rock in the Earth.

Magnetic field – the area of effect of a magnet (or the Earth) indicated by lines of force surrounding the magnet (or the Earth).

Malleable – bends easily.

Mantle – the layer below the crust made of molten rock.

Mass – the quantity of matter in an object.

Microorganism – an organism that can only be seen with a microscope, e.g. bacteria.

Model – a representation of a system or idea, used to describe or explain the system or idea.

Monocular – each eye is used separately to increase the field of view.

Monomer – a small unsaturated molecule that can be used to make a polymer.

Mutualism – a relationship that benefits both organisms.

Natural selection – the process by which organisms that are better adapted to their environment are able to survive and reproduce.

Neurone – a specialised cell that transmits electrical messages (nerve impulses) when stimulated.

Neutralisation – reaction between an acid and a base which forms a neutral solution.

Neutron – a sub-atomic particle found in the nucleus of atoms; it has no charge.

Nitrates – compounds containing nitrogen; plants need nitrates for growth.

Non-renewable – a natural resource that is being used at a faster rate than it can be made.

Nuclear – non-renewable fuel.

Nucleus – the core of an atom, made up of protons and neutrons (except hydrogen, which contains a single proton).

Nutrients – substances used in an organism's metabolism which must be taken in from its environment.

Nylon – a brand name of a polymer.

Orbit – the path of an object around a larger object.

Ore – a raw material taken from the rocks of the Earth from which important chemicals can be extracted.

Ozone – a gas in the Earth's atmosphere.

Parasite – an organism that lives off another organism.

Pathogen – a disease-causing microorganism.

Payback time – the time taken for insulation to pay for itself from savings made.

Phosphorescent – a chemical that can store light and release it over a period of time.

Photocell – a device that captures light energy and transforms it into electrical energy.

Photosynthesis – the chemical process that takes place in green plants where water combines with carbon dioxide to produce glucose using light energy.

Pigment – a coloured substance used in paints and dyes.

Pollution – chemical contamination of the environment and / or organisms.

Polymer – a very long chain molecule with repeating units.

Polymerisation – the chemical reaction where monomers are used to make polymers.

Population – a group of organisms of the same species living in a defined area.

Power – the rate of doing work; measured in watts (W).

Predator – an animal that hunts, kills and eats its prey.

Prey – an animal that is hunted, killed and eaten by a predator.

Producers – organisms that produce biomass when they photosynthesise, i.e. green plants; organisms that occupy the first trophic level of a food chain.

Product – a substance made in a chemical reaction.

Proteins – large organic compounds made of amino acids; needed in the diet for growth and repair.

Protista – kingdom made of unicellular organisms.

Proton – a positively charged sub-atomic particle found in the nucleus of an atom.

Protozoa – single-celled microscopic animals.

Pyramid of biomass – shows the energy flow through an ecosystem; always pyramid shaped.

Pyramid of numbers – shows how many organisms are at each stage of a food chain; not always pyramid shaped.

Radiation – electromagnetic waves/particles emitted by a radioactive substance.

Radioactive – substance that emits radiation from its atomic nuclei.

Reactant – a starting material in a reaction.

Receptor – the part of the nervous system that detects a stimulus; a sense organ, e.g. eyes, ears.

Recycle – to collect waste materials and make them into new products.

Red giant – a stage in the life cycle of stars – they expand to form a red giant.

Reflection – change in direction of a wave at a boundary between two media.

Reflex action – an involuntary action; a fast, involuntary response to a stimulus.

Refraction – change in direction of a light ray as it passes from one medium to another and changes speed.

Renewable – energy sources that will not run out.

Respiratory system – where gas exchange occurs, e.g. the lungs in humans or gills in fish.

Retina – the back of the eye; contains light sensitive cells/receptors.

Reversible reaction – a reaction in which the products can react to reform the original reactants under the same conditions.

Rusting – the chemical reaction where iron reacts with oxygen from the air and water to make rust.

Salt – the product of a chemical reaction between a base and an acid.

Seismic wave – the flow of energy going through the Earth after an earthquake.

Soluble – a property that means a substance can dissolve in a solvent.

Solute – the substance that gets dissolved.

Solution – the mixture formed when a solute dissolves in a solvent.

Solvent – a liquid that can dissolve another substance to produce a solution.

Specialisation – the development or adaptation of a particular body part for a specific function.

Species – smallest group/type of organisms; second part of binomial name. A species of organisms have similar characteristics.

Specific heat capacity – value of how much energy a material can hold. Heat required to change temperature of 1 kg by 1^0C.

Specific latent heat – heat energy required to melt or boil 1kg of a material.

Speed – the rate at which an object moves.

Steel – an alloy mainly made from iron and a little carbon.

Stimulants – chemicals that speed up the heart and nervous system, e.g. caffeine.

Sustainable – to maintain and keep in existence.

Synthetic – man-made.

Tectonic plates – the large sections into which the Earth's crust is split.

Thermal decomposition – the use of heat to break down a substance into two or more substances.

Thermochromic – a chemical that changes colour as temperature changes.

Thermogram – using colours to represent temperatures.

Total internal reflection – complete reflection of a light or infrared ray back into a medium.

Toxicity – how dangerous a chemical is to your health.

Toxin – a poison produced by a living organism.

Tracer – a radioactive substance that can be followed and detected.

Trajectory – the path of a moving body.

Transfer – moving energy from one place to another.

Transform – changing energy from one form to another, e.g. kinetic to electrical.

Transformer – an electrical device that changes the voltage of alternating currents.

Transverse wave – a wave in which the vibrations are at 90° to the direction of wave travel.

Universal indicator – a mixture of pH indicators, which produces a range of colours according to pH and can therefore be used to measure the pH of a solution.

Variable – something that changes during the course of an experiment/investigation.

Glossary of Key Words

Variation – the differences between individuals of the same species.

Virus – a tiny microorganism with a very simple structure.

White dwarf – a stage in the life cycle of some stars; medium-sized stars will collapse to form a white dwarf.

Yield – the amount of product obtained, e.g. from a crop or a chemical reaction.

(HT) **Benign** – a growth or tumour that isn't usually dangerous to health, not progressive or recurrent; does not spread all over the body.

Carbon footprint – the total set of greenhouse gases or emissions caused by an organisation, event, or person.

Extremophiles – microbes that thrive in physically or geochemically extreme conditions that are detrimental to most life on Earth.

Free electron – loosely bound electron in outer shell of atom which is able to move through metals.

Generalist – an organism that can utilise many food sources and therefore is able to flourish in many habitats.

Genotype – the genetic make-up of an individual, usually given letters to represent different genes, e.g. Bb.

Geology – the study of rocks and the structure of the Earth.

Heterozygous – to have different alleles in a gene pair.

Homozygous – to have the same alleles in a gene pair.

Hybrid – the infertile offspring of two different species.

Light year – the distance light travels in one year.

Malignant – a tumour that becomes progressively worse, and spreads around the body.

Multiplexing – method of sending more than one signal at a time.

Phenotype – the outward expression of a gene, e.g. blue eyes.

Red shift – lengthening of a wave as a result of an object moving further away in space.

Saturated – has only single bonds.

Smart alloy – a mixture of two or more metals, or of a metal and a non-metal, that changes its properties as the environment changes.

Specialist – an organism which has a small range of adaptations.

Subduction – a plate boundary where one tectonic plate is forced below the other and the rock melts into the magma.

Synapse – the small gap between adjacent neurones.

Thermonuclear fusion – the joining together of small atomic nuclei to make a larger nucleus; releasing energy.

Thrombosis – a blood clot.

Unsaturated – has at least one double bond (C=C).

Vasoconstriction – the narrowing of the blood vessels to reduce heat loss from the surface of the skin.

Vasodilation – the widening of the blood vessels to increase heat loss from the surface of the skin.

Key

| relative atomic mass |
| **atomic symbol** |
| name |
| atomic (proton) number |

| 1 | hydrogen | 1 |

Group 1	2											3	4	5	6	7	0
																	4 **He** helium 2
7 **Li** lithium 3	9 **Be** beryllium 4											11 **B** boron 5	12 **C** carbon 6	14 **N** nitrogen 7	16 **O** oxygen 8	19 **F** fluorine 9	20 **Ne** neon 10
23 **Na** sodium 11	24 **Mg** magnesium 12											27 **Al** aluminium 13	28 **Si** silicon 14	31 **P** phosphorus 15	32 **S** sulfur 16	35.5 **Cl** chlorine 17	40 **Ar** argon 18
39 **K** potassium 19	40 **Ca** calcium 20	45 **Sc** scandium 21	48 **Ti** titanium 22	51 **V** vanadium 23	52 **Cr** chromium 24	55 **Mn** manganese 25	56 **Fe** iron 26	59 **Co** cobalt 27	59 **Ni** nickel 28	63.5 **Cu** copper 29	65 **Zn** zinc 30	70 **Ga** gallium 31	73 **Ge** germanium 32	75 **As** arsenic 33	79 **Se** selenium 34	80 **Br** bromine 35	84 **Kr** krypton 36
85 **Rb** rubidium 37	88 **Sr** strontium 38	89 **Y** yttrium 39	91 **Zr** zirconium 40	93 **Nb** niobium 41	96 **Mo** molybdenum 42	[98] **Tc** technetium 43	101 **Ru** ruthenium 44	103 **Rh** rhodium 45	106 **Pd** palladium 46	108 **Ag** silver 47	112 **Cd** cadmium 48	115 **In** indium 49	119 **Sn** tin 50	122 **Sb** antimony 51	128 **Te** tellurium 52	127 **I** iodine 53	131 **Xe** xenon 54
133 **Cs** caesium 55	137 **Ba** barium 56	139 **La*** lanthanum 57	178 **Hf** hafnium 72	181 **Ta** tantalum 73	184 **W** tungsten 74	186 **Re** rhenium 75	190 **Os** osmium 76	192 **Ir** iridium 77	195 **Pt** platinum 78	197 **Au** gold 79	201 **Hg** mercury 80	204 **Tl** thallium 81	207 **Pb** lead 82	209 **Bi** bismuth 83	[209] **Po** polonium 84	[210] **At** astatine 85	[222] **Rn** radon 86
[223] **Fr** francium 87	[226] **Ra** radium 88	[227] **Ac*** actinium 89	[261] **Rf** rutherfordium 104	[262] **Db** dubnium 105	[266] **Sg** seaborgium 106	[264] **Bh** bohrium 107	[277] **Hs** hassium 108	[268] **Mt** meitnerium 109	[271] **Ds** darmstadtium 110	[272] **Rg** roentgenium 111							

Elements with atomic numbers 112–116 have been reported but not fully authenticated

*The lanthanoids (atomic numbers 58–71) and the actinoids (atomic numbers 90–103) have been omitted.

Index